BASEBALL AS METAPHYSICS

ALSO BY MARVIN COHEN

The Self-Devoted Friend

Dialogues

The Monday Rhetoric of the
Love Club and Other Parables

Fables at Life's Expense

Others, Including Morstive Sternbump

The Inconvenience of Living

How the Snake Emerged
from the Bamboo Pole but
Man Emerged from Both

Aesthetics in Life and Art:
Existence in Function and Essence
and Whatever Else Is Important, Too

How to Outthink a Wall:
An Anthology

BASEBALL AS METAPHYSICS

MARVIN COHEN

TOUGH POETS PRESS
ARLINGTON, MASSACHUSETTS

ISBN 978-0-692-96751-5
Tough Poets Press
49 Churchill Avenue, Floor 2
Arlington, Massachusetts 02476
U.S.A.

www.toughpoets.com

To Rick Schober, my rediscoverer;
also fan of my hated Red Sox,
a contrariness under neither
of us's control.

Contents

Foreword

This book is a reprint—except for title, cover, dedication, and this fore-word—of what was published in 1974 as *Baseball the Beautiful*. The then-publisher took the liberty of changing my now restored title, in order maybe to bring in the lumbering lowbrow audience who moved their lips when they tried to read, in the process dropping more clenched cig-arettes than they would have among today's surrounding cancer warn-ings.

By now both baseball and I have changed, the former changes being more publicly noticeable as an entrenched sport whose past and future literally dwarf mine, not just metaphorically.

Speaking of which, "metaphysical" thought is as natural as breath-ing, allied organically to psychological, sociological, philosophical, polit-ical, realistic, imaginative, surrealistic, and other such titular thoughts. So the original publisher need not have hastened to tamper with my title, if only he had known.

Too late, like many things.

Around 1974 the media implied that Hank Aaron was "controver-sially" challenging Babe Ruth's sacred lifetime home run record. By now, that "controversially" would have been stricken from public politi-cal consciousness as meaningless.

Today's baseball averages longer games and much fewer complete games from starting pitchers. Multiple relief pitchers dominate more of the later innings. The finisher had to go to finishing school.

Aside from the blessed topic of baseball, there's also life, and this author has been discovering that in my individual life, like baseball, I need more relief in my later innings. Some specialist left-handers are among some of my doctors, but they're supposed to think right.

The relationship between baseball and life is a matter of individual cases. You know who you are.

Another comparison between then and now, from original to reprint edition, is that today's players are increasingly recent, thus telescoping the nature of time, which is the plenitude we live by.

Geometrically speaking, the base-to-base and mound-to-plate proportions on major league diamonds have been so unchanged like Greek architectural classics from times ancient, that all we have to do to keep them that way is nothing.

Marvin Cohen
New York City, 2017

Introduction

Before I was a baseball player I was a baseball fan. Sometimes I think it was more fun to be a fan. And now Marvin Cohen has reminded me just how much fun it was. I remember, as a boy, journeying in from New Jersey to watch the Giants play at the old Polo Grounds. The joys were as many as the vendors' pennants I so coveted. Once I sailed a Dixie Cup lid down onto the field from my grandstand seat and it caught a current of air and, breathtakingly, sailed clear out to the pitcher's mound. I'll not forget that Johnny Antonelli, the lefthander, was the Giant pitcher that day. He picked it up, scrunched it in his hand, and deposited it in his back pocket. Suddenly I wasn't just an anonymous kid sitting up in the cheap seats. I was part of the scene. It was, after all, *my* Dixie Cup lid. Therefore, *I* had moved Johnny Antonelli, as surely as though I had slammed a line drive back at him and made him leap for his life; a thrill, something my brothers and I talked about for months. Speculation: for how long did Johnny Antonelli carry my Dixie Cup lid in his pocket?

That's what Cohen has reminded me of most, I suppose: that overwhelming desire to be something more than a faceless fan, to somehow become part of the action, to become important to it. When the Giants won in 1951 they didn't do it alone. I had won too. When I went to school the next day, I strutted as though I were Bobby Thomson, as though I had hit the home run. And, in a way, I had. Hadn't I *rooted* for them? It was almost the same as Johnny Antonelli picking up the Dixie Cup lid. My rooting had caused the Giants to win. Ergo, I was a Giant and entitled to bask in the glow of their victory. "Come through, Lord," Cohen writes. "Guide us through the season. Lead us into the path of righteousness, and triumph. Otherwise, you're fired!" Exactly. On the other hand, success is deserving of reward, and part of it is to strut the day after your team wins the pennant.

Of course, Cohen is a superfan, and he has written an intellectual manual for his co-religionists. They know who they are and they will cherish this manual. But anyone who has spent a soft, green afternoon, his shirt open at the throat to the sun, the whistles and chatter of the infield drifting up to the edge of his mind, watching, absorbing, taking in a baseball game, will cherish it.

Perhaps no one who has ever played the game could be the kind of fan Cohen is. Not that he is a little-boy fan. He would never, for example, slip into the trap of thinking that the old baseball players were better than those of our time. Yet he knows why so many people want to think so. "Each man's golden age is the year of nostalgia he is most loyal to," Cohen says. Again, he is precisely right.

No ballplayer ever understood the game on the same level as Marvin Cohen. Me, I never knew there was anything metaphysical about baseball. I just knew it was difficult. The ball was round because the world was round, maybe. In which case, I wish the world was square. You can throw a much better curve if you've got a corner or two to grab onto. Still, I easily detect the cry that is just beneath the surface of almost every sentence of this book: "Life is hard to handle; it's too enormous. But baseball is in a neat, confined package ... There are *ways of entering it.*" The cry of the fan. I understand it so well I am surprised I could ever play the game. Perhaps I played it well for so short a time because underneath I am as much a fan as Marvin Cohen.

Jim Bouton
New York City, 1974

The Baseball Season's Latest Birth

The baseball season starts again. It's the same one as all the others, but with some players gone and some new ones in there, and some same ones but older: like your own body this spring, with some cells gone and some new ones in there, and some same ones but older. But baseball is going to outlive your body.

All previous seasons, like a serried chorus of ghosts, congregate at the opening of this one, like all of a tribe's grandmothers assembling at the first birthgiving of the newest bride, drowning the midwife with instructions from all surrounding directions.

This season is an unfilled form, a huge vague opening out of various unknowns and potentials. Day by day, bit by bit, its blanks will be filled in, as outcome after outcome issue into the aggregate of an over-all hierarchy of climactic results: division winners, pennant winners, world champions, pitching leaders, batting leaders, stolen base leaders, fielding leaders, all the way down to trifles and to dubious, negative record-breakings. All this is to be, bit by bit, in unfoldings, unfurlings, game by game, as trends develop and comparisons become revealed. All this is not yet, but it's just starting, the bare and pure beginnings.

Beginnings are pure, because possibilities can be idealized, hopes unsullied. Dreams ride high, and preside over beginnings. It's the fictional enchantment of the dawning awareness of love's bond, complete with free-furled promise of all conventional enthralled bliss: engagement and divine betrothing.

For most teams and players, too soon will "the honeymoon be over."

But now, all is possible. Young and old fans rule, for what they imagine is as yet undisputed by the doings on the field. It's the hopes' early triumph. It's the self-blessed promise, confirmed and endorsed by the same self-fulfilled act, of proud imagination, before the season starts contradicting in earnest, indelibly recording actual balls pitched, missed, hit, caught, thrown, real plays that comprise real innings cumulatively decisive of the games themselves, entered into permanent record books.

Some hopes will prevail, and be proven forth. Let the many plots thicken, and shape a strange new drama.

And shake off old ghosts. All previous seasons, who preside over our latest birth—get off our backs! Don't intrude or mock from your privileged boxes of tradition. Let our newest season fill its own sweet, bitter being out, by itself—deemed "destined" when the future looks back on this as a multiple, complete, and final act.

Baseball Praised: For Its Objective Self, Measurable and Clean-Cut, Balanced and Precise; and for Its Accommodation to the Imaginative Subjectivity that a Fan May Personally Place on Its Altar

Like a tree, baseball is a thing of dignity. A tree knows how to balance itself, roots in relation to trunk in relation to the outspreading and the growth. Pitcher battles a balance, with all the fielders on his side, against the wood-wielding enemy. The distances are right. From pitcher to batter, from base to base. There are enough chances, there are enough accidents, and when those things even out, it's still a test of skill. What it comes down to is that the batters with the most talent have the best records. Ditto with the pitchers. Baseball tests ability. Out of it all, an archives, a legacy of records, of statistics, has come down to us. And the compilation is always going on, season after season.

Merit on the field gets accounted for, is registered. What one does extols or condemns him. Baseball is eminently *fair*.

Performance tells. You can look it up. The home run wasn't hit because the hitter's father was the vice-president of the team or because the hitter married the manager's daughter. The no-hitter was pitched with no quarter given, by token of no favor, in getting all the breaks by being born and bred on the right side of the tracks and having the right table manners and college accent. The pitcher did it himself. He *earned* it. Baseball is purer than life; it's symmetrical, fair, and dignified. There's no debating what happened: it happened.

It happened: concretely, empirically. So much so, that the intangibles, the spirit, are the presiding halos over baseball. Records make for legends. Baseball is our great national myth. The crowd roars in unison, or those of it that have in common the art of being the same team's rooting fans. They all pull together. Enthusiasm, hysteria: a common love. Baseball is bigger than us all. (But you have to love it to look at it this way.)

"Immortal Diamond"—a phrase of Gerard Manley Hopkins. The diamond treats all men as equals. On one corner of that diamond stands a man. If he's fleet enough and gets a fast break, he might steal second. Or he might score, on a given hit down the right field line. In the latter case, the right fielder's arm might have a deciding effect.

Baseball is a game of inches. Fair or foul, safe or out—what happens, happens. It goes down into the record book. And records don't lie.

The structure of baseball is its art. It's a structure that admits of infinitely complicated possibilities and combinations, within the rigid framework of rules in common, of distances to fences, of worked-out angles, of human proportions. Man is the measure of all things. The Major League ballplayer is the measure of the distances on his field of trade. Given these, he must do or die, win or lose. It's the majesty that dignity imparts.

Proportions and measurements are the poet's tool, the sculptor's trade. And they rule in baseball.

Baseball needs no defense, or reason for being, beyond the joy it gives. But it can also be a corrective for too much immersion in modernity's topsy-turvy disorder. Let the hypothetical victim of that disorder here advocate baseball's therapeutic purgings, in a grateful testament which speaks for many in these uneasy times:

I plead for baseball, not because it parallels my life and adds another cool dimension that corresponds to the larger smoothness of my baseball-like life. No, I plead for baseball because—as a brilliant invention and development of an objective, verifiable system—it's an imperative antidote to my life which is totally the opposite. My life lived in New York City in this middle part of the twentieth century is a muddled, muddy confusion, with no law or form, with no standards to operate by, with no absolute values: it's an anarchy of the hodgepodge, my life, without any determinate guide or goal for resolution. Therefore, I embrace baseball, with its intricate possibilities of clarity that a fixed form can confer. I *need* it, it soothes me, it gives me bigger visions of a possible ideal harmony along a living order. I thrill to it, I'm emboldened by it, I feel more noble.

It makes a bigger man in me, at least in possibility, it unflags me to a firmer sail of higher contemplation, and gives optimism a chance.

John Keats, the English romantic, wrote: "As tradesmen say everything is worth what it will fetch, so probably every mental pursuit takes its reality and worth from the ardor of the pursuer—being in itself nothing." In another place, he referred to "Nothings which are made great and dignified by an ardent pursuit."

Thus, this book of enthusiasm about baseball can only appeal to the one already converted, to those who have been blessed with comparable feelings. Delights are not really transferable, or transmittable, to those they're not "for," no matter how strenuously we labor to point them out or however enticing our recommendations appear to *us*. Things are only taken by those who need them. The seeds of the importance of something must already be growing in the appreciator when he meets the outside thing corresponding to the seeds and crowns it with the rush and interlocking of recognition. Thus, the baseball fan likes baseball— he endows it with himself. To anyone else baseball remains nothing, unbrought to life.

Baseball reaches out and affords a haven for our most private subjectivity. We can imaginatively project, and become, the ballplayers we admire. The game is what we read into it. It affords such scope for our self-glorifying ruminating by proxy, a window-shopping for performers to identify with, performances that are done for us, if only we spend the transforming enthusiasm of fancy in return for so handsome a human pageant.

The world has been changing. Society has become technological. To balance that, we've at the same time become more deliberately mystical.

Statistics, a weight of sociological details, scientific data, political trends, economic graphs, all the charts of calculation, all the process of geometry, all the mathematical ratios: they've necessitated that we cultivate a pseudo-Buddhism, to defend the spirit against numbers by stressing that all numbers are One.

Hence, baseball is one myth. The more records and percentages deluge him, the more the fan's ardor becomes extraecstasied. The spirit balances the intellect, to keep up the human proportion.

Baseball appeals to the immortal in us. Thousands of ballplayers are listed in *The Baseball Encyclopedia*, and already most are dead. The game of baseball continues. Life's the sport, with a new season to play. (Robert Coover made this clear in *The Universal Baseball Association*.) We're outlived, and outplayed, by what's vast, which survives us. Art does this. And baseball, too.

The nineteenth-century players had face hair. In the 1940s the players were clean-faced. Now there's hair growth again, in frillish styles. The ballplayer with the thousand faces, like Joseph Campbell's *The Hero with a Thousand Faces*, repeats an archetypal pattern, in historical cycles. Time is bound by one ballplayer. He is all heroes, whether his name be Honus Wagner, Walter Johnson, Yogi Berra, Ted Williams, Willie Mays, or the ones known only to the future. He's anyone who ever played, who ever put on a glove and spikes.

In fact, he's *all* ballplayers. Like life, baseball depends on mediocrity. Mediocrity is the base on which brilliant records are achieved, the performances of lasting fame. There's an average mean, statistically. That establishes a scale. Those who rise above, we can see how, and by how many degrees. The great man is above average. His feat is extraordinary. He lives in the undying record book. He's unburied, and lives in the human mind. Never mind how long ago he did it: he'll survive.

That's how classics live, in literature. And baseball is the bold parallel.

The Ravings of a Baseball Fanatic

Life is a mystery. We're always verging on new unknowns; also, we're continually poised on the same *old* unknowns. Nothing gets permanently solved.

So it goes in the great mystery of baseball. There are temporary solutions, fabricated conclusions, makeshift arrangements: a pennant winner in this league for this year, and one for that league. They fight it out, they go at it, for the World Championship. One of them is bound to win it. For the loser—as for all losers—"Wait till next year."

Tentative champions. There's no permanent hold. The immortal trophy is "retired" with nobody. It's newly up for grabs next year.

The issue is in doubt. What to happen next. The unknown outcome. We're in the dark. We're a theater audience. The decision withheld till the end. Crescendo: a conclusion always in the making.

Opposition. Polarizing. Clear-cut opponents. Symbolized by the uniforms. Rivalry. Enmity. The difference in uniform. *Ours* are all white, in pinstripes, blue stockings, et cetera. *Theirs* are all in gray, red trimmings, et cetera. We'll *beat* them. The enemy is *identified*.

In fact, it's like warfare. Them against us.

A battle to the finish. Our men against their men.

The rites of battle. The rites of war. The rites of spring. The rites of *sport*.

Yes, I'm part of my team. I *root* tor it, don't I? So I've invested interest. I want return on my investment. I've committed myself. I'm loyal. So I expect *something* in return. It must be joy. My team's fortunes are mine as well.

I go along with them, through thick and thin. Like a marriage contract. Except this is a marriage of the *heart*.

True, it's a one-sided marriage. But they—my team—don't know it. It's all on my side. But it's sweet. Sometimes sour: when we lose. But that's life, I suppose.

My team, for good or bad. (Like, "My country, right or wrong." Or, "My wife, in sickness or in health, for better or for worse: still tied to her.")

Yes, you lose *yourself*—but what you gain!

Yes, you've momentarily exchanged your private, dull, personal ego for something big, impersonal, ritualistic, symbolic.

You're now *more* than you. You've merged with your team, you're one with it. You've merged with the body of all the rest of the team's fans: you're one of them. You're a ... fan.

You belong to a group! You have a corporate, a collective, identity. You're no longer "just" you.

Rave on, fan. You're mad!

The Poetic Wellspring at Its Purest on the Youthful Field

On the sports fields, schoolyards, and empty lots of our boyhood, people were at their spontaneous best, with a natural zest, full of humor and fun; without trying, they were that way, as they were or were to be nowhere else.

When young and idealistic we encounter, in playing sports, something that answers to our natures the craving for the poetic, the lyrical. There's something wholehearted in the atmosphere—something pure, transcending—that remains for many of us grown-up men the pinnacle of delight.

There's something in the back yard or sandlot or makeshift ballfield that corresponds in a free-flowing, rhythmic, physical way to our truest, unvoiced ideals.

The guys we played with—they were never to be the same again.

Truly, those were "the good old days."

Then, in the country of the grown-up, you search and search in vain for the semblance of them—for the free flowing of boys at play. For the spontaneity that came together just that once.

For us, there was poetry in those times. We tasted of some ideal—indescribable.

Man is at his best when young, and on a playing field. Physical lyricism, rapture—something perfect in the air is caught. It's to become the archetype for poetry in his life thereafter.

He turns in nostalgia for that elusive whiff. He retains it inside him—it's never lost.

Spring, summer: on the playing field. Life flows ahead, forever.

Growing Up Along with Baseball and Acquiring an Old-Timer's Scale of Pure Nostalgia

Almost any American male has in his emotional memory the times as a boy of feeling "how he rated" among the other kids in competition, if not in actual sandlot (for those now middle-aged) or Little League (for those who are still young men) baseball, then in those youthful variations of baseball—softball, stickball (with a pink rubber ball or tennis ball), or other derivations or improvisations depending on place of play, number of guys, and equipment on hand. (The wonderful, inventive makeshifts, both conventional and inspirational, of energetic, creative, sports-loving youth!)

An American male will remember his pride and prestige when promoted to the "varsity," or the like; or in some glittering performance that comprised his finest hour. And he will remember the sorrow, the disappointment, in realizing the realistic limit, on any lot, field, or schoolyard, to his hopeful aspirations of one day "making it" to the Big Leagues—everyone's dream, and punctured in competition.

Such disillusionments are still being compensated for years and years later, in fields of endeavor ever remote from the purity of baseball itself.

Baseball is built into a lifetime. Whereas the kid has a current hero to "look up to," the old-timer venerates the past "great ones" in the Golden Age.

Each man's "Golden Age" is the era his nostalgia is most loyal to—when his sensibilities were being intensely formed, and the world was new, radiant, significant.

The delightful love and labor of a lifetime is baseball if you grow up along with it and feel its annual rhythms with your own. This lifelong romance, full of its sweets and sours and ups and downs, parallels your other lives over the same stretch, and in miniature reflects your total life.

It took all of Proust's life, in the living and the writing, to do his huge work. Baseball too demands a whole life, and rewards your compliance with illuminating parallels to everything else that's gone on in your life. It's a gauge or framework, a touchstone, affording interesting correspondences to just about anything else. There's a natural network of these connections running through each live baseball fan.

Year after year goes by. You get older, things happen, events change, and there are new pennant winners, new world champs, new batches of stars rising or in their prime. Each baseball year can be a landmark for your *own* life; you tell time accordingly. You were one person *before* that amazing World Series climax, and afterward you went into a new era, you left college, you had *that* job, you went with *that* girl. And after so-and-so had that record year, you were married. Thus, baseball aids the memory of one's own life; season after season, year after year, it's all going on: together—you and baseball—in dexterous counterpoint, sustained perpetually.

Simultaneously, you and baseball interweave your threads throughout years and years. For *your* lifetime coincides with particular baseball years, that fill your mentality with images of the players and events in the unfolding tapestry, the annual pageantry, contemporary with your awareness. My life and baseball have gotten mixed up, deliriously.

You "go through" it all. You pick up memories along the way. For the old-timer, anything new of interest in the current season is really a "touching off" of some precious old memory in some comparative way. He "lives in the past." But that's glory he lives in.

The older your memory, the more purely evocative (rather than for its own sake) is what's current. My, how those old-timers can reminisce! given just a touch of what's latest on the field. They're driven way back and come up with gems, newly polished for the occasion.

The lifelong fan has simply "latched on": baseball is a gold mine. He's drawn in, absorbed, obsessed, like a lover who simply can't get enough of his new girl. All details glisten with significance in this enchanted zone. The fan is "hooked," he's an addict. His fixation becomes an enriching of other areas of life, since intensity in one field, like baseball-interest, is infectious; other activities and interests "catch on" the conflagration, in an all-pervasive contagion that perks up life's tone, from one aspect to another.

Conversely, dullness in one area tends to spread its atmosphere, to permeate into other areas: then, all of life gets bogged down.

Life begets life, liveliness generates liveliness. Enthusiasm is the key. When it's for baseball, then that level can apply its keenness to art, literature, history, politics, friendship, marriage, parenthood, a job, any involvement: you're on fire. The fire went to baseball, and it leads from baseball to anything else. Don't let it be put out, life is too precious.

Life permeates, spreads itself. It takes many forms, baseball is one.

That old-timer doesn't even have to "keep up" with the latest doings. He has the whole past to feast upon and even to give him a sense, through osmosis, of what's occurring today. His background is an impeccable guide, through infinite perspective, toward "rating" by proportions in a solid scale all new players and events. (Of course, he may downgrade the new ones out of loyalty to "back when." But grant him that, it's human.)

He's naturally conservative but generally fair in his estimations. He admits that the new things aren't so spellbinding as those blessed peaks he wears so devoutly in pious observance. He's *married* to those peaks. They were his halcyon honeymoon, he's bound to them, they were paradisiacal glimpses his heart never recovered from—gratefully. He romantically preserves the memories. This is pure sentiment, enlisting what we call "spirit," "soul," "heart." It's an act of love. Love errs with excess. But love is worth every excess. It's life spilling over, into eternity.

Dreaming Into Baseball

Dream into the open spaces of the baseball turf, even if you're not there at the park. You're there anyway.

Dreams projected into green waste patches, reveries musing on the field. Lots of emptiness between the fielders, to post your billboard daydreams, and see what's not there.

Same with cricket: three-day county matches (11 a.m. to 6 p.m. each day, with lunch and tea breaks); five-day international test matches, lots of time and green space, the open sward, just to dream down upon. (That's if you're in England, or Australia, West Indies, New Zealand, India, Pakistan, or South Africa. If not, then be in Japan or the U.S.A., where there's baseball. That'll do.)

Like the opera fan at the opera dreaming upon the wondrous sounds, or between them, the baseball fan "reads in" what he wants; those somnambulant motions down on the field permit the fan's fantasy to knit itself blue and pink, at length, yarn and all.

Some of that fantasy is woven upon the real game, if there's no better competition that the head privately offers. And what's wrong with the game itself? Plenty there to get your hooks on and bite into.

Man *tampers* with what he sees; he becomes part of its truth, for in tampering he sets his own mental stamp upon the proceedings and endows them with his own pure visionary stuff. They wear his magic coat-of-arms.

The players can personify what we want them to. Some are contemporary gods to boys and men. Others represent something less glorious, beyond what they actually are and do.

The fan has the lot to choose from, to cast his being upon whomever he selects. It's all down there before him. The possibilities of his own reality—his secret aspirations and well-nursed frustration-triumphs—are magically laden upon the diamond and the choreographed figures there. It's a special world.

Identify with the batter and first base beckons. Identify with the swift runner taking his lead off first base, and second base stealingly beckons.

Identify with the tall central figure on the mound going into his slow windup, or taking his stretch motion with a runner on base, and your point of view is shifted again. He's your focus now. You share in *his* world.

Some humble fans modestly choose only average players, not especially distinguished, to identify with.

An advantage in this is unique possession. Few or no other fans have "confiscated" these "average" players. The fan who does take an ordinary performer has him exclusively for his own; his loyalty may be rewarded should that player's stock ever rise and he get better in late career; then the fan rises with him, with the satisfaction of having been there from the beginning, staking unpopular barren pioneer ground for his own and finding his choice vindicated over a patient trial of time.

But still, the fan's averageness was projected, at least, into the charmed circle of the Major Leagues—an exalted dreamzone of great rarity. For whom do we know who ever made it? Though everyone dreamed about it, and all uniformly failed.

The fan may feel shut out, alienated, with a dim job, no prospects, and a lousy family life or none. Fame and fortune's worldly favors go to others, never to him. But there's consolation: the nonluminary workaday player, picked for identification, lends a special glamorous objectification to the fan's dismal lot—a more brilliant dimension, a sparkling magnitude. The fan is raised to a corresponding grade on so vaster a plane—it's the Major Leagues! The level is immense, and the fan leaps in his imagination. He's transported, and transcended—redeemed: his other self is playing there.

Even not being a star there, just having made it—it's like touching Napoleon or Jupiter and eating meals with them. Just "being in the same league" with them: now that's a climb, and there you are. By extension, you're far beyond what you really are. You're lifted by your humble hero. And who are those "immortals" who call him colleague? They have clay feet. They're accessible, through him.

The world loves heroes, envies them, tears them down. A "working stiff's" social status can get vicious compensation when the hero muffs one or pops up in the clutch. "There, see, no one is a god. Okay, so *I* flub; *I'm* human, too."

Thus, inferences are drawn. The myth is all there. The fan picks out what pertains to himself symbolically, in working out his problems and doubts by finding ultra-self matter to externalize fantasy for his own secret purposes. The fan is welcome. The players have no notion. They just go on, with their *own* problems—just as real. They, too, resort, for fantasy, to spheres outside their reach. They're like the fan too. But they're well-paid athletes, that's all. They have their own careers to struggle with. Their world *is* baseball, by action. The fan's at his passive remove—but he's in there, hitting and tossing, as well. With *him*, it's all mental.

Getting a slant on the whole scene through identifying with one player: like getting an angle on the entire world by just being only you— one person.

Just as a whole historical era can be revealed in focusing on one character in that era (as eighteenth-century Britain seen through Boswell's biography of Samuel Johnson), so too all of a current baseball era can be lit up, in background and perspective, through a fan's devoted following of his special hero.

Fickle fans switch allegiance. "What have you done for me lately?" They're resilient, drop yesterday's hero if he's stopped "producing," and take up today's darling. Such fans, herdlike, often conform to trends in *general*, not just as baseball fans. How they behave about baseball is a good indication of how they are in general. How *anyone* behaves about baseball can reflect the way he is in general. A man's baseball attitudes can be taken as a measure of him as a whole person, within a psychological framework of consistency. They're *free* about baseball, more off guard, with their hair down, at leisure, looser—thus affording a reliable betrayal of their truest selves. For example, a fan who argues without regard to accuracy may reveal a slackness in intellectual approach in other areas. All his traits tend to extend to his baseball mouthings-off as well, and so show him as he is: he's unmasked to reveal even what his masks are, and disarmed so that all his armature shows. His humor is more evident, in his role as a sports fan, and humor can window his whole soul in one casual exposure, if you seize it. Observe the baseball fan—see the man himself, beneath.

The achievement of excellence is a thrill—to hear about, read about, or watch—whether as a short-inning performance, or in a game span, or in a whole season, or a career. You feel for that performer: it stands out, what he did, as beyond his own accomplishment, and it now belongs to everyone. Excellence becomes collective property, as a universal phenomenon. The vicarious sharing is a bond between people, as beauty in art, which touches a common chord to unite all beholders alike under the instigation of an ideal touched into life. It pervades: beauty, excellence, the truly well done. It's not begrudged, for we're all participants in something so elemental that it's too rare for the performer alone to hoard; it passes into everyone's legacy, and can be opened right now, beheld and remembered. Prized, one of our great landmarks. Our hats are off. A member of our own race did it: a tribute to humanity.

Picking sides, picking a winner, or picking a favorite. Or picking *your* favorite—even if an underdog.

Belonging to something. To go up and down, *along with* the rise and fall of the fortunes of a team that's yours—for better or for worse, through thick and thin. You stick by it, and what happens to it becomes part of your life. You're drawn outside and are more than merely what happens to you personally. You're invested in a whole team venture: its very uniform is yours. You love your team, hate to lose, love to win. Your horizons are theirs, and your boundaries soar when the going's good, shrink in when the team is losing. Your ego is enlarged: a whole team is feeding it. It's interesting. You want to live long, to go through season after season with them, and hope to put together a winning streak. When your team is in the pennant race—you're intimately right there with them, and your support is spiritually alongside them, to urge them on. You periodically rip through yourself, and lose your personal concerns, in your fan interest. These "vacations" are welcome. You come back, we hope, purged.

To watch a game ("live" or on TV) while rooting passionately for one team is a totally different experience from watching the same game without a rooting interest. The former is like watching your own son play competitively—how can you be neutral?—while the latter is like watching strangers play, with no participant calling forth any emotion. "Indifference" can be a base for fascination, too. Serenely you observe, and soak it in. Nothing is at stake. You feel like God that way. Impartiality confers a sense of being "raised above." You make your dispassionate appraisals, calmly knowing that nothing bad will happen to *you* anyway. Let those poor souls fight it out. You're at a safe distance from that fray; you're spared trouble and concern, given the luxury of peace, independent of how things turn out there. This security can't last. You'll have to face your own life again: troubles and doubts will rear themselves, and snaky anxieties squirm at you. But let all that wait. Look at that nice play! A fine catch! How delightful! Keep yourself entertained. Your escape is congratulatorily brief. Enjoy it while you can. What's the score, by the way? Three to two? Oh, whose favor? Really? Who's ahead in the standings? Ah, now that's interesting. The race is close. Only two more weeks to go. Well, too bad *my* team is out of it. I'm resigned to that. So I'm calm now. Oh, look at that! A *great* play! Who made it? Who? Never heard of him. A rookie? Well, I don't follow the game anymore like I used to. Not since my team has been so consistently low in the standings. I don't care who wins, now, as long as *my* team can't. But the year will come, again. You bet. Then I'll be like a boy again. Everything on the field will excite me. Then rooting will be fun—but with the risk. Now it's useless to root. All they need is a new double-play combination, and a strong lefthanded-hitting outfielder, and a dependable starting pitcher, for them to be in contention again. Well, I'll wait for that. My life has plenty more years in it. My team will start a new dynasty. Then my *own* life will make a comeback. I'll be a new man. I'm in a rut now. But I'll snap out of it: my *team* will show the way.

A man is in a slump, or his team is in a slump. He gets them confused. That's natural, for his *team* is him, just as *he* is him. The team is sort of a hopefully ideal self. May it prosper! Then, if all is not well with *himself*, at least there's *something* to hold up his pride. He can always point to his team: like a poor immigrant factory-worker father taking refuge and compensation in a son doing so well in college that he'll be worth thousands in a flourishing profession upon his triumphant graduation. The *team's* the thing/whereupon I'm king!

Yes, I have to hedge against pain, by being indifferent as a fan when the risk is too strong and the odds too great against my team winning the pennant. I weigh my team's chances. If it looks like they may "make it," then—but not till then—will I dare to really root vociferously, like a maniac. For, oh, I must not fail!

An old Yankee fan, in recent years, has had to put his wonted arrogance into mothballs till his day comes again. (Will it ever?) It's too agonizing to crash against futility in hoping vainly, till the greatness shall recoup itself. Hence the current reign of austerity for the once-proud Yankee devotee: resignation, humility, proscribing of lordly hopes, reconciliation to a spell of limbo; renouncing cherished ideals to lay low awhile till the reality will correspond with them in spring and renaissance. Meek now, but to reinherit—in time—the rightful Earth: pennant and World Series. Pious submission, then great wrath, deliverance, vindictive redemption: to slaughter the usurpers like Ulysses upon his homecoming to Penelope and Ithaca after losing his way at sea following the victorious conclusion of the Trojan War.

Does the word "fan" come from "fanatic," or "fantastic," or "fantasy"? Yes, it's related to all of them, by derivation. Baudelaire in his prose poem said that man should always be intoxicated on something: the sea, the moon, a woman, wine, a book, a friend, *something*. The *fan* is intoxicated. He goes into a frenzy. He's in love, with his team. Or he loves life, or he loves himself—and takes it out on the team by taking the team *in*, to his heart. Rooting is affirmation. It's to bless, and hope. To pray: to win. And if you win: elation. Bliss. Don't mention the alternative, that is, to lose. It's not positive to think that way.

Oh, to dread to lose. Losing is despair. Losing is more than losing, it's worse. It's extreme negation.

Lord, bless my team. Take them through the whole pennant race, but put them out ahead. Make them World Series champs, to cap it all off. Then I'll believe in you, Lord. This is a bribe. Give my team the flag, and I'll be a believer. Come through, Lord. Guide us through this season. Lead us into the path of righteousness and triumph. Otherwise, you're fired!

That was my ultimatum to God. He let me down, I turned atheist. But one season he'll win for me. How devout my piety shall be! For I'm a true believer—but only if I win. The name of the game: Win. The strife is for that.

No man is an island. He's also his team. The man is but inside. The *team* comes inside, too. Especially certain players. Then what they do outside *matters* inside. For the inside is composed of the matter, and cares what happens. Care is the heart's function. Then a man is not alone. His team and certain players *count*, his heart has a use, it goes out, incorporating them. They're carved in moving relief, on the man's final being. He loves and hopes. There's dread, anxiety. He's *living*, feeling these. He's *on the team*, he's in there pitching. The game isn't over. His life isn't over. Each game, each season, *is* his life. His one life, and he the only one living it. It's that one team, against death, in one game, in one season. It's going on. It's not over.

A Meditation on "Ball"

When a ball was invented, it revolutionized one of man's necessary spheres: play.

It sure was a glorious day, once the ball was invented. What was it in imitation of?

The sun, a globe, the planet itself, the moon when full, and the earth's irregular rotundity (polished regular). But play dictated, or prescribed, a necessary condition governing the nature of the ball: it had to have the property of the *bounce*.

Yes, man insists on humanizing his playthings. His toys must conform to the image of the use he puts them to. Man hasn't the patience to abide by accidents: he lacks the passivity. He molds, constructs, alters, remakes, transforms, and creates. Then, his playful toys can work for him, for his ideal pleasure in hard-earned recreation and much-sought leisure. A premium value is attached to play, in its perfected artifice as highly regulated games, polished by exquisite application and tradition, a professional refinement of athletic competition. Man is *particular* about his mode of play: so much so, he's become mainly a spectator. To please us, the performers must develop extraordinary skills. They must even break records with miraculous performances. They must be exceedingly adept at handling "the ball," whether with the hand itself, or racket, or bat, or club, or glove, or whatever instrument may come to hand, depending on the sport.

The ball is a thing of beauty. Its sphere is symbolically duplicative of the earth it's played off of. Man creatured the earth, and domesticated such regularities as this ball, because man loves games and he wants standard rules, so that records may fairly be set and the record book respected. So the curvature is regular, the playing field meets specifications, and the uniforms are stylized, in formality.

The ball's the thing: the outfielder is chasing it, as it rolls to the fence, unimpeded. The pitcher is about to be "relieved." The bull pen will release the reliever. The pitcher had gone too far, letting the hitter hit one too far. The game being in the balance, the pitcher can't be trusted; now he's just yielded another hit. Two runs are in, the score is tied. The pitcher is headed toward the showers. It's the "ball's" fault, not his. The ball can dictate its own terms. It felt lonely for the solid contact of "wood."

Goodbye, pitcher. Congratulations, batter, standing on second base, with two brand-new runs batted in to his credit. He was lucky the ball needed the bat's solid thump. He loaned his wrists to assist in the impact. And fortunate, too, that the ball seemed placed *between* the outfielders, and not on a line to one of them for a well-hit but sickeningly wasted "out."

Ball, you have a life of your own. You pick your favorites, don't you?

But it evens out, sort of. The batter won't always enjoy such a feat. Sometimes you'll aid the pitcher, and, leaping from the bat, feel lonely for a glove without a bounce, won't you, ball? And you'll nestle into some nice fielder's glove. So warm and protected there in the pocket, after the brutal shock of your exposure to the open force of such a vicious bat.

Nice Ball. The new pitcher is surreptitiously moistening you. If detected, he's guilty of the "spitball." But now you're up to flying tricks, Ball, you swerve, like a butterfly, all slimed with dew. The batter is cursing you, missing you. He's out, strike three. You rounded-out little imp! You mischievous, two-timing, fickle Ball! You favorite-player on all sides, you half-controlled, half-whimsical, arbitrary little center of being! Wherever *you* go, eyes follow. In flight or in bounce, where *you* go, Ball, fortunes rise and fall, bets are won or lost, championships decided. It all rides, Ball, on you.

You're replaced—a foul was hit in the stands. But your replacement is still you. He has your same bounce, density, and spirit, standard of dimension. All balls are one ball. And one ball is all baseball; and what sweat, skill, curses, prayers, go upon you, Ball, from the men who professionally touch you with hand, glove, bat, urging you to do the tricks on behalf of the self-interest concerned. But you're neutral. You do your stuff, you strut. Generation after generation of players take turns with you. You're live, Ball. And life goes into you. Years of carefully nurtured professional training, by the best surviving competitors that try their hand at the game. They know you can't be bribed. Big, big fields can barely contain you. You fly all over the place—mainly from pitcher to catcher. You're our globe, our globe is a baseball. Is it being struck by a bat, in outer space, or is its orbit being curved for strike three to a huge outside catcher's mitt? Hold on. The world is in progress. The game is in the balance. In the laps of the gods? In the hands of the players. Playing gamely, but for keeps. It's cosmically more than a game. It's all of planetary life, on the velvet turf of sheer astronomy in infinite durations. Cells die on the ball, the clinging germs that are dusted off, in the ball's progress, like people on the earth. The ball is in motion. The ball lives. The players? Mere adjuncts. They exist, perhaps, as courtiers of the Ball, that Prince whom they follow, imploring, conjuring, devotional, obedient, patient, like trusted advisers each staking his own fate on the curve or bounce the Ball will take, arbiter of destinies, but given to arbitrary sulks and fits itself. The Ball—a creature of caprice, a mover of men, a mounter of scores, a decider of contests, an apportioner of careers. What a heavy burden!—but worn lightly, in the air.

Appreciations for Simple Things

A ball is an arresting object. It's magical and universal. The great thing about it is that terrific property it has: bouncing. It's suitable that baseball should be played with a ball. What would the game be *without* that spherical object? Plenty lacking, that's what.

The ball may be pitched (by the pitcher), thrown (by any fielder), caught, dropped, fumbled, chased (by any fielder), and hit (by the batter). Thus, the ball's versatility is without dispute.

It even employs real people for its multipurposes. Grownup men, who get paid for it. With admission charged, too. But the ball conducts its enterprises gratis; its only reward is the fun it's having making real people go through all those complicated motions, for *its* sake. Like a dog controlling the actions of its "owners," setting them through their paces, even affecting how and where they live—for *its* sake. But the ball is a *benevolent* despot, and does, after all, *spare* people. It has compassion for the player. It *tries* to be consistent, and *seems* to be obedient. That fools lots of people—but unmaliciously. There's always a winner— even though, alas, there's a loser, too. Like those gods who had to decide between the Greeks and the Trojans, and took disputing sides in controversy over the raging outcome, it's the *ball's* whim to hand the winner's apple sometimes to *this* team, sometimes to *that*. Of course, skill counts too. (That is, the skill of the players themselves, those semi-puppets of that puppeteering arbiter, the ball.) Players are allowed a certain leeway of independent action, by the ball's authority, in a limited monarchy. *Do* give the players credit. It's not *always* the ball's fault.

Bad bounces are part of the game, and accidents, the unaccounted-for, which may "turn the tide." A ball can go high or low, in varying angles of trajectory and degrees of velocity. Whenever it goes up, it always comes down, due to gravity. Thus, most pop flies are caught. (If they're not, they come down anyway.)

Most of the time, the ball *can* be controlled. Practice gives predictability to the bounce, over which the fielder can have mastery. Which, provided he can hit, raises his salary.

Thus, good fielding pays off. But sometimes the ball just "gets out of hand," for a vital miscue. In such cases the official scorer might or might not give out the "error" sign, for such a costly fielding lapse, or for what, after all, wasn't the fielder's fault. But anyway.

Of all the sensual delights in the world, none has a purer ring than the impact of the connection of bat and ball. This sensual instant is the batter's continual paradise: when he "gets a hold of it," and really "drills" it. It's the welcome thump of triumph for the bat craftsman. His human ear is resounding with an angelic chorus. (Provided the ball "falls in there" and is not caught. If the latter happens, he might utter an oath too foul to quote here.)

The resounding crack, the solid contact, the pure unreasoning immediacy, the well-cultivated sensation. The batter's joy, the pitcher's woe (assuming it's a safe hit); and the fans are all divided, depending on "which side." Anyway, tumult.

Fun is the name of the game for fan and performer. And via simple things.

Fielding is a "chore," compared to the natural joys of hitting. But beautiful, routine acrobatics can swirl in the field. With the ball flying over the green turf, or bounced into a double play, marvelous reflex motion is called for. The fielders are lithe and agile, and their gloves have glue in them. Fielding artistry.

The bat is lovely to handle. The golden willow, the majestic swish of the ash, the tapering curves of it, still or when swung. The length is just right, and the weight. Wrist action is essential, in the art of batting.

The man on the mound pitching, with his assortment of "stuff." The catcher crouching, giving the sign. The batter "digging in," bat on shoulder, waiting. Here's where eternity focuses. Here's what it comes down to.

Crack! It's a hit! And it's going through! The tying run is coming in to score! It's a new ball game!

The crowd roars, naturally. It's summer pleasure. It's the North American Twentieth Century of Civilization. This is popular, mass culture. Season after season, it endures. It contains *some* universal, for such appeal. It releases something within man. For what's so festive—or solemn—as play, the pure spirit of play?

A Ball Game as a Self-Designed Artwork Pushing Through Time to Its Form

Like literature, music, opera, theater, and the dance, baseball takes place in time. (Architecture, sculpture, and painting don't—they're purely spatial.) The performer and the observer, while a game is in progress, look back and look ahead: the present action is laid out in a shifting, dramatic time field. A rhythm, of sorts, weaves its way through the "accidents" on the playing field. A current play, involving positioning and decisions, is affected by what was previous in the game, and is having its effect of what's to come later; the game may be seen as an organic unit. Every pitch has its place in there, somewhere.

The game in progress is a structure-in-the-becoming; if you see it, through time, as a whole, all the separate episodes can come flashing together, and interlock, to shower aesthetic illumination on a drama of its own devising.

This is to see baseball as an artwork-in-the-making affair, totally unrehearsed, improvised by more than eighteen men, who thrust in their various skills while the moving parts pass through innings, highlighted by crucial plays, to the conclusion being thereby created.

At any one point, there's anticipation, deliberation, preparation: "Now" is a building-up. "Now" is never only for itself. It's cumulative "progressing," in strife, to form the game's unfolding. Nor are any two games alike, any more than two artworks that push themselves into being through the resistance of time, incident by incident, in head-on conflict by two complicated machines designed to win through accidents and opportunity. "What's happening" is contingent. There's a whole game to be gotten through.

The Chance Factor, in Tight Games, for the Graying Manager, or for the Headlessly Bellowing Fan, in Different Ways of Being Moved by the Fair or Foul of That Ball After Heaven and Earth Are Moved to Anticipate What Turned Out to Cross into the Unknown with That Strange Air of Surprise

In baseball, if one thing doesn't work (you being the manager), you try another. There's no one mechanical system that gives unfailing results.

A game comes to be a "scrap," dog-eat-dog. Then you play it by ear. You consider all the situational determinants, the unforeseen, and see how it's going, since you couldn't have reckoned on these unaccountables and made any "game plan."

What's actually taking place, play by play, in the funny way the ball bounces, the reading of the fluctuating situation, getting in or out of a jam or hot water, being in position to—

It varies, so you improvise, as there's no quite figuring the dope sheet, not in advance, since surprise dictates.

The course of a game alters in a tight contest; sometimes it "see-saws back and forth," and you move the shortstop over, or bring in a lefthander to pitch to the lefthander, or go for the hit-and-run, or put the "steal" sign on, or go for the sacrifice, or bring in a pinch-hitter; or you deliberately walk the slugger with first base open to set up a double-play possibility even though— And once making these decisions, then you leave it to your men to execute, and you pray.

In *War and Peace*, Tolstoy contrasted Napoleon's style of generalship with that of the lesser-known Russian general, Kutuzov. Napoleon had an intricately contrived, preplanned strategy which he'd stick to, being the conscientious military professional that he was. The result would be that sometimes he left himself no room to remanipulate in event of something previously uncalculated. The machinery, already in process, forestalled possible changes of maneuvering that might become suddenly advisable.

This rigidity would sometimes turn out to be a blunder for Napoleon. The Russian general, being more flexible, was able to seize opportunity upon the unexpected and, whatever "came up," he could turn to expedience just as he saw fit, since the mold wasn't hardened. He was able to take advantage more of changing troop moods, weather fluctuations, terrain discoveries uncharted in maps, and other intangibles that happened to come his way as possible crucial factors.

The Russian general, accused of slackness, won the battle; Napoleon, air-tight in meticulous deliberation and with a firm omniscient grasp, lost. Chance plays its role, and sometimes it's a dominant one.

"You never can tell." "The ball takes crazy bounces." Clichés like these abound, not only *in* baseball but principally *out*. The weight of experience attests to good reason for this.

There's a tendency for "tight" contests to be "broken wide open," or to remain "touch-and-go." Odds tend to even up, the game is balanced toward the dramatic—that is, kept in the balance, result withheld till the end, the team behind catching up, the team in the lead being caught from behind, the scales shifting evenly.

The unknown is up ahead, you encounter it as you come to it, it becomes a *contest*.

The gap is narrowed, the score gets tied—"the game of inches" can explode, either way. One team has the edge, struggles to keep it, sees it slip away, and "It's a new ball game!" as broadcaster and telecaster Mel Allen used to announce jubilantly, cornily intoning it Southern.

The manager drives his team to win, it's his business. The fan—except the extremely loyal one—is free to be a prophet, pick the winner, be an expert predictor. The manager is at the helm, or in the driver's seat, but his job is at stake, so he's ulcerous with responsibility. The fan has the luxury of both rooting with partisanship and soberly "seeing what the score is," even dispassionately. He can indulge exultation or depression on a crucial outcome, but essentially go on unaltered, as before, in his ultra-baseball life.

To win is the object. But the drama is that that goes for both opponents. So, expect a tussle. The game ain't over yet. No, not by a long shot.

The game in progress—the lead reduced—the manager plays a hunch—what's gonna happen next?

Yeah, it's not over till the last man is out. And even then—the rancor, regret, and debates keep that contest echoing "what if—?" in the locker room, the manager's office, the bus carrying the tired fan home, or out on the porch with the television set finally cooling off. "If only—" "Yeah, but then he would have—" Endlessly, there being no proof. Plenty of room, here, for irrational likes and dislikes, emotional indulgence for favorites, against misfavorites, just plain griping, or sounding off, wager arguing, bets paid off leading to enmity, boasting, grumbling, saying anything. No need to check on it too close, it's not science; the uninformed's opinion is as good as the expert's, or just as confident in its swagger-statement. It's a way of being drawn close together—even banteringly, mock-pugnaciously, or whatever the manner—with others, with groups (or in a pair) of any size. Or even with yourself, the pros and cons. There's always *another* day, and a new game. No need to modify your prejudices, you can air them anew anytime you like—if you're a fan.

But the manager grows wrinkles, prematurely grays, and—as he feared—is fired anyway. The breaks. If only his ace starter hadn't hurt his arm in mid-July ... Well, there's religion for consolation, if need be, and drink for the atheists. Life goes on. It's only baseball.

Baseball as Scale and Structured Language to Articulate Everything by Its Coded System, Enhancing the Significance of All That Falls Within It

Human society in the big world at large is so sprawling and amorphous (despite sociological strata, classes, and subdivisions that endeavor to tidy up all the chaos into recognizable parts of a concentric whole), that it's hard to seize upon extraordinary things and mysteries. *All* seems extraordinary—or dull, pointless, without aim—when there's no comparison system, no stable base against which to single out, separate, and evaluate amazing specifics from their dressy counterparts.

To put it another way, the world has no *scale*, being lumpen and shapeless. Everything is thrown together, without order: no rhyme-or-reason scale to discipline it.

Without a scale, we can only be subjective, and deluded, about what *seems* incredible, or about what seems to be anything: there's no basis, or criterion, to go by. Mere information doesn't *fit* anywhere.

But baseball (like other organized sports) *has* a scale. Thus, we can pin things down, with a rule of comparison. Thus, nothing is lost that happens in baseball, for all is accounted for, down to the minute dimensions and catch-all network of the Scale.

The Scale in baseball has just the right size and light structure for judging anything that happens in an "overall" light. Nothing slips through the net.

A man's personal scale is too small or singular to judge phenomena by. The world's scale is too vast, bulky, unwieldy, to judge phenomena by. But baseball's scale is just right—not too flexibly loose, not too rigidly tight—for seeing what happens, within baseball, as a baseball thing. An event adheres to the language, or terms, which baseball sets up. It falls *within* a system, and can be *placed*.

Baseball as grammar, vocabulary, syntax, structure—rules for understanding, for all the people concerned, not just in one private man's fantasy. A preventative against "madness." A "rational" system, for sanity, since all agree upon it, the known premises and processes. All baseball fans, however scattered in space and time, speak the same language. It reassures them, and fortifies their "belonging." They're a "breed" apart.

They have a language for translating the mysteries that fall within their special scope. Thus, all the mysteries are seized on the wing and pinned down in the baseball dimensional world—a *structured* world. Relations and degrees are seen, and clarity emerges.

The game produces mystery made manifest and palpable. (Mystery exists when we can see it; when not tangible, it's ethereal, improbable, speculative, unfounded, vague, too personal.)

The ballplayer is always watching mystery; he has a *vehicle*, a *form*, for looking for it, so he's able to see it every time and appraise its wonders. It's *open* to him, due to his finely closed system that has a place for all things and illumines what enters it.

World society, not regulated by rules as baseball is, lacks a form by which to discern and read and render "actual" its own mysteries.

The overall human mystery of man within the inexplicable world is bigger than any individual's life-size, but is at the same time smaller than the ultra-confounding cosmic mystery that extends beyond man and the global locale he futilely ponders.

Life is hard to handle; it's too enormous. But baseball is in a neat, confined package—it's *compact* in its complexity. There are *ways of entering it*.

The world being so many-sided, so apparently, invitingly, but deceptively open, there are no agreed-upon conventions as "ways" of "getting at" the things that sloppily clutter, bulging and overflowing, the world that "contains" them.

Baseball, on the contrary, is *full* of conventions. You enter it, you "get at it." It's a "packed" delight.

Similarly (as Francis Fergusson pointed out in *The Idea of a Theater*), the French theater at the time of Molière and Racine had definite stage conventions, agreed-upon artifices to standardize procedure in a sufficiently common backdrop as to render more highly dramatic and discernible any slight variations in the stage action.

There was enough of a uniform "constant" as to delineate and make vividly dramatic the special qualities of the variables.

Thus, there was a form for judging by. It took the spectator out of the world and placed him within the *finite, known* boundaries of the theater conventions peculiar to that time, place, and culture.

This gave the spectator eyes. It was a uniform enough, stylized, artificial world, so that anything that happened within its confined, deliberately rigid, austerely formal dimensions could be *seen, felt, realized* for what it was, placed within the prescribed code. Each detail or variation or trembling nuance in the deeply circumscribed action became absolutely significant—with an enhanced mystery made manifest, carried out, truly acted.

And so with baseball, in its own way. It takes us out of outer chaos, removes us from the formless worldly confusion, and conveys us to a set arena, formal and precise. We're placed square in a well-defined system that renders visible, actual, palpable, each and every varied mystery that happens under its rules. Its universe is well-timed and orderly.

That's the virtue of "rules": it means we have something to go by. It's fair and equitable, as all the fans have something solidly in common as a starting point for their perceptions.

Then, when they argue, at least their disagreements, however far apart, have proceeded from some sanity of basic agreement. They have a mutual base from which to fly apart in contention. Their arguments, then, can refer to grounds. They all start from the same premises and proceed from mutual assumptions common to all their tribe. Baseball's system of conventions provides a fine family union among all the fans.

So too did the French theatergoers in the time of Racine and Molière have this advantage of assumed fundamentals, stereotyped effects, ritual procedure. It sophisticated them, to make confident allusions and inferences which wouldn't be lost upon the initiate. The ground rules were well known, yet it made them feel exclusive, "in the know." There was solidarity among that audience: flattering to each, stabilizing, reassuring, as a fraternity should ideally be whose members feel at one. And understanding circulates; intelligence can make fancy leaps from assured positions.

Assumptions held in common can be liberating. Confinings help the individual to become unconfined, for he has a place to return to. He can wander, for he has a nest.

The concept of an "academy" carries this unifying goal and advantage. Agreement first, based on a common law. A structure for inventive variations.

The quibblings over particulars can be carried out on that structure. There are areas for "working things out." It's "civilized."

Tribal conformity is a primitive, though often-cultivated, example of this. The tribal members are linked in spirit. There's a *bond* running through, to draw upon, for sustenance and safety, in confidence and serenity. The *sharing* is ungrudged—though it be only principles that are shared. *Upon* the sharing, deviations can go unworried.

And so each tribe member can appreciate, or anyway recognize, the mystery a fellow may point out. A similar orientation makes their seeing communal.

In a same true sense, baseball fans, though they live apart in time and space, and most of whom are destined never to meet, constitute a definite community of minds. They inhabit the same baseball sphere, whose circumference is at each fan's center. Its roving round universals are a penetration of mystery by a conducted language. Those outside the pale don't know.

Primitive Superstition, Religious Helplessness Before the Unknown: The Farmer's Analogy

The nature of baseball and of the kind of life it necessitates makes the ballplayer religious, or almost religious—or at least compulsively superstitious, which might be a chief component in religiosity. Not right away, perhaps, but it will incline the ballplayer to become this way.

For one thing, there's much that's ritualistic about baseball, from arriving in the morning at the clubhouse to don the uniform and perhaps to change the tape on one's sprain, to the beginning of the game, throughout the whole process of the contest, to its conclusion—and afterwards, back in the clubhouse, changing into civilian garb.

Day after day, or night following night, there's an incessant repetitiousness, as relentless as a continuing drumbeat, as compulsive or compelling as a rhythm, as hypnotic as a rite.

All that routine, as a deadly or lively background to the unpredictables, the surprises, the daily accidents, the unusual occurrences, the unexpected, the amazing, that always somehow happen.

And the ballplayer has no control over the surprises. He can't account for them, or be on his guard in preparing for them. Some of them are mishaps that could be costly, costing his team the game, or even him his career. And in the face of a surprise, he's impotent from preventing it happening—as unable to avert his disaster as to anticipate it. Then, all is over.

Since the origin of man, the tillers of the soil, the farmers, have traditionally and proverbially been of a conservative and religious temperament. It's by the nature of their occupation that they've been so. Just as it's in the nature of the baseball life.

For one thing, the farmer and the ballplayer do all they can beforehand to prepare, to sow, to till, to keep in shape, to practice, feed the livestock, lay by provisions, oil the glove, sharpen the spikes, et cetera. The most advanced methods, tools, techniques, paraphernalia, et cetera, are resorted to and practiced with. The muscles are gotten in trim with training, and the coordination sharpened. Then, finally, all is left up to—chance!

The locusts might come to spoil the crop, or the player may be "beaned" and his eyesight irrevocably affected. The frost might come too early and spoil the crop; or the ballplayer might twist an ankle sliding and be hobbled for the remainder of the season.

Because of the unexpected that looms or hovers over, there comes the tendency and habit of prayer, of muttering vows or oaths to ward off the worst, to bring on the best: a bonus crop of base hits for the hitter, a bonus crop—period—for the farmer. This brings on a religious mentality.

The farmer has no power, is not equipped, has no provisions to avert a drought from the unpredictable heavens—day after day of unrelieved sun to dry up the soil and parch the thirsty seeds, the harvest is killed off. Helplessness, if God should turn wrathful. Nor has the player any potency beyond his mortal professional properties to overcome a trick of fate on the field that undermines his confidence or binds him from "delivering" in a crucial clutch. "It's in the hands of the gods—pray, boys."

The farmer and the ballplayer learn to appease the heavens, to propitiate the gods—however primitively, crudely, unorthodoxly, or by the most private of superstitious, eccentric behavior. They know how finite is even their well-rehearsed ability, which any celestial prank can outmaneuver. No guard keeps away the unforeseen. Accidents overcome the great, the talented, the cunning, the resourceful—even the previously lucky.

One's fearfully inadequate limitations turn to the heavens to appeal to the omnipotent. Omens and divinations try to out-trick fate and read favors. To soften the wrathful gods to mercy, superstitious acts are inaugurated, which repetition converts into devout nervous habits.

Thus, a certain manager will touch third base every inning, or have his wife keep wearing the same hat till his winning streak is stopped. Or a pitcher might wear a religious medallion. Or the coach will mutter incantation mumbo-jumbo at specified intervals. Or something will be "tried": invented, odd, queer, quirky, obsessive acts to allay anxiety and court the concealed bride of fortune.

This is due to uncertainty, insecurity, as the occupational hazard of baseball life. There's no automatic scientific cause-and-effect process. Nothing is assured, not even through diligence, vigilance, alertness, keeping in shape, constant practice, et cetera. The unknown keeps stealthy, treacherous, coy, fickle; this balances inordinate pride. Farmer and player bow before the unknown; they're humble, by caution and sore wisdom.

When human humility increases, the gods' arbitrary power over those humans increases also, at the same rate. Or perhaps the latter caused the former. Mystery inspires awe.

Players and farmers are aware of the *gamble* factor involved. There's just so much they can do—then they hope. And by hope, I mean: to entrust to the gods the power—mysterious—that mere humans lack.

Hardened veterans, grizzled farmers, learn best. They "can't do it all themselves." The displaced willpower (or free will) defects to God's portion. The farmer and the player *dare not* be too proud, for the gods have punishment in store, which had better not be tempted.

The field of play as a church: or two contending churches, of the same denomination. Interlocking factions, in "the hands of the gods."

Rite and Play: Mime and the Release From the Workaday, a Purging in to Play

Baseball is two opposite things at once: it's an escape from one's life and reality; and it's a reflection of one's life and reality. In its latter capacity, it affords a new peculiar "play" perspective or slant into one's everyday life and events; it's potentially symbolic of a great many aspects of "real" life. It's based on something—not carved out of thin air. It *refers* back to one's life. (As well as *getting away* from one's life.)

Likewise, in a primitive tribe, when the day's work was over, the hunting and feasting finished for the day, there were fireside ritualistic dancing and chanting, which did two opposite things: *reflect* the tribesman's day in symbolic reenactment; and *divert* from the tribesman's day, affording relief, release, entertainment, so that he might forget, momentarily. Both functions work together: he forgets rememberingly, he escapes into another consciousness of what he's escaping from. He achieves a catharsis by seeing the familiar, repetitive workaday in a "plaything's" new light.

There's *miming* of the day's motions; and the miming is a pleasurable motion in itself. It's play-acting, and goes into what it gets away from. It repeats, but ornately, with leisure and delight, what was hard work and routine. It brings forth, brings out, and transcends into joy.

Miming and the spirit of play are very close, perhaps one.

Play is another version of work, voluntary and minus the drudgery. The same ingredients as in work are in play, too—but in a more enjoyable form. "Art imitates life," said Aristotle. Art, imitation, miming, play, rite, reflection, repetition. It brings things into a more palatable light, and restores perspective.

The purging of excess, the curing of annoyance, making fun, mocking, aping, being critical, creating equanimity from anguish. Sanely balancing the ordeals and dreary spots of life into brighter patches, deliberately constructed. The human will, in its guile, helping one "come through." Finding a way out, into fun.

To affirm, and brighten the negative.

Transformation from reality to fantasy—which is a new, perhaps keener, version of reality. Transformation into new terms, into grace, dance, comedy, and the poetics of delight. This is man's tribute to himself and the bearing of his burdens in lighter garb, in rich forms of play.

Going crazy, going wild—in disciplined, rhythmic patterns. The buoyant spirit of release.

The intoxication of abandon. Comic resources, to embroider what's tragic and to express what can and can't be done about the insane condition of living, working, and dying. Play: man's brightest creation.

The lyrical, the ecstatic. The broad, the funny. It's artificial, it's by man—we adorn nature with this, and it seems natural. It is natural, for we made it.

Pagan, Ritualistic, and Religious Resemblances to Plain Old Baseball

To make living more neat and tidy for a change, we like our emotions to be identified with events, clearly. This, baseball can provide. What's happening there on the field is symbolic only of itself, if you want to have it straight. Or you can have it straight and multirepresentative at the same time. (Like T. S. Eliot's phrase "objective correlative"—the closest style-form approximation, verbally in metaphor, to a feeling or idea. Or like James Joyce's non-Catholic, pagan concept of "epiphany"—an event that seems to represent in compact intensity many similar events of the same nature.)

We need dramatic objectification of what's otherwise an untidy rag-bag of our cluttered feelings. Baseball can sparkle by presenting what's clear-cut. Definite things take place, on the field, unambiguously, before your very eyes. This cleanses and purifies our overcomplicated internal lives: a cleanly objective experience is tangibly happening, and you're the recording witness who will be able to refer to it specifically in memory to other sane, rational beings, or on the spot, if they're seeing it immediately too on television or in the stands. You can't argue with what *is*. It's there.

Nice for something to be real, for once. It makes you believe that there's *some* order in this world. Just a segment of it, there, on the field. Still, it gives you hope.

Baseball is a form of ritualism like a religious ceremony. So is bull-fighting, with rituals before the actual blood event. Japanese wrestling is also ceremoniously observed, like a Mass or something.

Baseball, going on, seems courtly, ceremonial, with many noneventful intervals in its spasmodic, unflowing rhythm of slow deliberation. It's methodical, yet haphazard within that. There are swift bursts of action, abruptly blurring. Then, another stretch of routine dullness.

These contradictions and inconsistencies are somehow held in bounds by the stylization and formality of the rite procedure. Devout fans attend this outdoor act, with devotions sometimes blasphemous or sacrilegious, but nevertheless conforming, however loosely, to the customs and observances of the pious gathering. It's an "occasion." It didn't just happen, it was *scheduled*—like Mass is, for a Sunday morn.

In ancient Mayan civilization, there were crucial ritualistic ball games before spectators of graded ranks, played with the brutal imperative to *win*. When the often bloody game was over, the losing manager or coach was "sacrificed"—that is, put to death on an altar to the gods, in a solemn ceremony no less religious for being pagan.

To pursue the religious analogy with baseball to the inside of the game, away from the fans' view: Baseball has a closed-in administrative structure, like the Church. It abides, like the Church, by its own tradition. The Commissioner of Baseball is in some ways like a Pope. He exerts his own personality on administration, sometimes severely, like Judge Landis, sometimes more leniently, like more recent commissioners.

To preserve its traditional character and identity, its cocoon-like ingrownness, baseball depends on the reserve clause, which binds a player to the team that "owns" him. If more players like Curt Flood resist the reserve clause and such time-honored baseball laws, it would be like Catholic priests rebelling over the chastity clause, in a trend toward the increasing secularization of the Church. Can the Church survive partly secular? Can baseball adjust to a more liberal organization? The world is changing—even radically. Conservative bodies like religion and baseball—can they be essentially altered by the radical sweeps and still retain their true natures? For these dual or unified answers, consult the historical future, which exceeds the scope of the writer limited to the "present," which is always never up to date, always falling behind.

Baseball seems to be a monolithic, tradition-bound structure, like some rigid military organization whose inflexibility would render it obsolete when conditions change. But baseball seems somehow destined to endure. Will it endure in a form similar to the present, or different? Young readers will have enough years left to one day know; old readers will die in the sanction of uncertainty, alas.

Aggressive, Hostile, Offensive — to *Win*. Belligerence by Rules. The Warring Instinct at Work

The pitcher is invading the batter's territory with a maliciously flung ball, and the batter wishes to settle the score. This is warfare, hostility.

The fan hates the enemy pitcher, being a fan of the side that's up at bat, and he identifies with the batter in a sublimated, vicarious, refined sadism against the hurler. To destroy the pitcher and ruin his career, to ruthlessly pile up a huge lead, is what's wanted.

The batter is aggressive. But the *pitcher* aggresses as well—and may even throw *at* the batter, attempting to knock him down or back him up from the plate, so intimidating him that he no longer dares to "dig in" with that sure toehold and confident air.

In baseball, the "attack" means the batting. The "defense" is the pitcher and the fielders. But in cricket, the "attack" is the bowling (pitching), while the batsman (batter) "defends": he defends his wicket, to keep the bowled ball (almost always bounced) from hitting any of the three stumps he's "defending," which would have the penalty of his "losing his wicket." But, of course, the batsman may "defend" aggressively, with a variety of vicious "strokes" (in any direction—there are no foul lines) to score as many runs as possible.

In cricket terms, a "hostile" attack means that the bowling is good and effective, taking "wickets" and preventing too many runs.

Though the batting side may compile a huge total of runs during its lengthy "innings," the batting is still the "defense" in this eternal warfare.

In football, the defensive platoon tries to crush the offensive enemy's attempt to score. Soccer has terminology similar to football—"attack" is "offense," for scoring thrusts at the goal; "defense" is to frustrate the attack, keep the ball "out of the nets," take the ball away from the enemy and begin an offensive maneuver yourself toward the goal at the opposite end. In basketball, "offense" and "defense" are also ever at odds, changing sides in changing tides, back and forth.

There's something belligerent about wanting to win. It means actively depriving the other side of a victory. It means to *inflict defeat*. It means to *beat*.

Baseball is peaceful warfare, though, compared with *real* war. In that respect, it's infinitely superior to the "real thing."

There'll Be a Decision: The Sense of an End Swaying Thought and Deed While the End Is in the Making

A baseball game almost always ends with a winner and a loser, thanks to the extra-inning clause in the good old rule book. But a cricket, hockey, or soccer match, and less frequently a football game, may easily be drawn and end in a tie.

The assurance that there'll be a definite ending—a result, a conclusion—is a strong factor in the psychology underlying a baseball game.

One team must "die": it's foredoomed. The only uncertainty is *which* team.

A man's attitude to himself and his life and to the world is vitally conditioned by his "sense of doom of an end." It makes him hurry up to make the most of his finite time here and play up the factor of his having a prime. Man takes less for granted, thanks to his mortality. He seizes on things, he's eager to reach out and find importance and significance in whatever, which he won't let slip by without his clutching hold. He knows the end is nigh.

He knows it's tragic to be alive. The pagan Greeks and Romans expressed this tragedy. But for the true Christian believer, there is no tragedy, due to the afterlife myth as redemption for the soul in another league, the ultimate of salvation—a higher league: the Majors, in fact. The devout Christian, then, needn't despair about the tragedy clinging to mortality; an immortal career in the Big Leagues is hardly a tragic end, as every theologian will agree.

Baseball would be played differently if there wasn't the foreknowledge that the contest will come to a *decision*. It would be altogether a different matter if there could be a draw, or an indefinite protraction without an end in sight.

The time factor. A novel must end (using death or marriage as conventional solution-conclusions), a life must end, and so too must a game. (Not to mention the long season.) We read the novel accordingly, live the life accordingly, react during the game or season accordingly—whether as a player or as a follower. Our attitudes are dictated, strategies and philosophies determined, by time in its absolute ruling essence, casting its moving shadow over events before us. A hovering or overhanging, a suspending, ready to sweep down. This spirit pervades all we do and see; it's the mental blood we swim in, or that circulates in us. We feel "something in our blood." It's uncanny. We're heading toward ...

The final score, in a game. The standings of the teams at the climax of the season to finish the pennant race. And the World Series result. It glares at you. Mortality in triumph. Mortality in defeat, too.

Baseball: still another reflection of time's mysterious current. A discipline and demonstration of it, both in the performance and the observation. Inning by inning passes by, play by play, pitch by pitch, game by game. And then, the statistics.

The Ballplayers' Sociology: Belonging on the Field

Fans visualize a game from a mental above-the-field level: whether actually in, or imagining being in, the stands, which is where fans are placed.

Players, on the other hand, visualize the game from down on the field, which is quite a different level of operation.

So obviously, fan and player are rigorously divided by what different conditions and atmospheres there are on the field and in the stands.

Players, by being on a special ground or field, feel a special relation to other players. They all *belong* there. They're part of a well-paid professional exhibit. There's dugout camaraderie, clubhouse understanding, linking ballplayers as a special breed apart, which non-ballplayers are unfit to understand.

People reside in separated apartments: we live apart from each other, except at work.

The field is where the players work. Theirs is a special line of business. They're united even with players on other teams. Their isolation is only private—off the field. Private life isolated into apartments for residence. The career world—join the fray.

Putting on the uniform—and a man has his place. The ballpark, the diamond, are his fields of operation. He's paid to be observed. His is an open performance. Other players are in a similar predicament. So their bond is a natural one, through working conditions. That's where they are: that's what they are. Who? That's a private matter, underneath the layers of publicity that expose the ballplayer.

The sociology of a ballplayer on the field, as opposed to the surrounding world of non-ballplayers who naturally never belong on the field. It's peculiar, being a ballplayer, and having this special place. He understands other players, they're part of a breed apart. The uniform makes the man, and the field confirms him.

The Tragically Short Span of Excellence; the Brief Term of a Player's Fading Glory

Baseball reverses the ordinary business-world life in one respect: age of most valuable worker. Doctors, lawyers, politicians, servicemen, executives in all walks of commerce and industry, in advertising, public relations, finance, construction, science, education, civics, journalism, publishing, the creative arts, et cetera, are generally more successful and more highly paid when older. Whereas, baseball is a younger man's game, and the young ballplayer must quickly strive for a high salary, knowing that his career in excellence may indeed be very short—he must make the most of it in a hurry, before he gets "over the hill" and is benched, traded, or sent to the Minors.

Hanging over him is the insecurity of a probably limited term of "holding his own" against increasingly tough competition. This is generally true too of the fashion model, the prizefighter, certain types of movie or theater actors, the dancer, the fashionable singer, and others in precariously short-term professions that face competitive and trend hazards in seasons of necessary brevity, after which they're displaced in turnovers by newcomers with youthful energy or newer techniques.

We "normal" folk go on all our lives the same way, more or less. The ballplayer has a double life, in that his best, most vivid years of success are soon over. His is a more precarious, glamorous, dramatically fluctuating, limelight-foreshortened life, for that reason. He's soon expelled from his eminent perch, and his glory must fade into an old-timer's memory.

Thus, not only do we non-players view the emerging young star with envy, but also with pity, in our foreknowledge that he's necessarily riding for a fall, and is "doomed." We see in his professional height our own overall mortality. There's philosophical and poetical irony in contemplating the few admirable years as they're passing by, of a diamond hero. Similarly, the Athenian audiences of the classical Greek theater viewed the doomed hero strutting proudly on the stage with his heroic *hubris,* regarding his pathos with pity and terror, with ironic detachment, knowing as he didn't know that his fall from glory was fated, pathetic as inevitable, to cut him short in his mightiest stride. This was the heart of tragedy. So too are Hamlet, Othello, and Lear tragic figures. As spectators, we see our own lives equally doomed. We pity the noble performer not merely with ironic detachment but with compassionate involvement. We're spectators, participating in the participator's destiny: inevitability has a note of sad finality much in common with us all, the watched and the watcher. The watcher is not superior or more fortunate: he has temporarily an added awareness. Then misfortune will topple him, too.

Tradition: A Base for Appraising

Baseball being a definite setup with rules, a self-enclosed system backed up by historical precedents and based on solid tradition, anything unusual that happens on the field may immediately be detected, since it departs from ordinary custom and from average "norm." Any record-breaking performance is at once taken note of. Or any feat *approaching* a record, like three consecutive strikeouts by a pitcher, or five runs batted in by a hitter in the same inning, or two assists by an outfielder in the same game.

Any deviation from the "usual" is noted, since every baseball-knower knows what the usual is, and has that same "usual" in common with all other baseball fans—as a standard, a framework, a reference, from which to judge each new play, game, or season's performance.

Similar to that is the great "common law" body of law precedents built up through the ages in any country, giving a judicial base on which to fall back in analyzing and estimating any new case. Time and many cases preserved in records have made of the law a *structure*, a body, or institution. The compilings and accumulation of related data, in an extensively ranged system with ample official documentation, compel confidence via established authority.

Baseball, as well, is a venerable institution. Its archives are very extensive indeed. It has its own museum; its historical process as a continually evolving body is a legacy to generations of Americans.

In 1961, Roger Maris' sixty-one homers were a phenomenal accomplishment, since Babe Ruth's sixty in 1927 had been a precious landmark much preserved and celebrated. So when someone new came along and had the luck, talent, and presumption to *top* it!—well!—controversies flamed. The reactionaries and tradition defenders (most old-timers) cited that the Babe did his in a 154-game season, whereas this new upstart Maris had the benefit of the modern elongated season, et cetera. Thus an asterisk was appended to Maris's feat in the record book, with its explanatory footnote that qualified Maris's "breaking" of the record. The Babe's legend thus became safely preserved.

Baseball is monumental, for it contains many monuments, to and of itself. Like Babe Ruth's monumental 714 career homers. Like—too many numerous examples abound.

And now, Henry Aaron between 1973 and 1974 is one home run behind the Babe's record. As the 1974 season opens, all eyes follow Aaron's every swing. His significance is nothing without the deep body of hallowed tradition and legend constructed through the ages of baseball behind Aaron's monumental topping of the feat few thought could ever be equaled. Thus, baseball challenges its young: and sets up the young, by allowing for new great quality to gain the pure importance imparted by extensive background. Quality emerges, in the depth of intricate comparison.

And the comparison notes that Aaron had many more times at bat than the Babe, and that the Babe's *rate* of home runs per times at bat is much higher. Still, Aaron deserves better luck than Maris, by going asterisk-free in the immortal record book. And so he does. Comparisons can't be *too* precise: quantity and quality sometimes tangle. The numerical is somewhat arbitrary. Both Aaron and Ruth are in baseball's heaven. Heaven is no number-observer. It deals with essences, whose purity is untarnished by the quantitative. But below, facts shout against facts. Which facts do you want to emphasize? Depends on what point you're trying to make. So the fanfare never dies down. Argumentative wagers are staked. Baseball is a growing body of history. And history is interpretable. The interpretation alters, with each controversial now, which offers its immediacy to the open market of all that ever was. Aaron's *adjective* is Ruth. The latter modifies the former. But Ruth, in turn, has himself become modified, and newly interpreted, by Aaron's rash "deed."

History absorbs Aaron, and mixes him of the same blood where Ruth flows. History is still hungry. It's got a lot of eating behind it, to *follow up* on. The bigger it's grown, vitally, the more new sustenance it needs. So the future is *already* competing. There's infinitely more room, the more there has already been.

The Innumerable Angles, Each a Total Focus of Vision: Varieties of Views Reflecting on a Central Touchstone

Insofar as "the medium is the message," baseball is an entirely different game from different avenues of reception. (More conservatively, I would say that the medium *modifies* the message.) Anyhow, baseball is one thing when you're playing it. Subdividing that, it's far different for you if you're pitching than if you're in right field. And baseball is another thing if you're in uniform but on the bench. Then, baseball is quite another thing altogether if you're a spectator watching from the stands. Subdividing that, it's a different game if you're watching it from the boxes back of a dugout—compared with watching from the mezzanine back of home plate—compared with watching from the bleachers. Baseball is another thing altogether if you're watching it on black-and-white television, and still a further or different thing if you're watching it on color television.

Then again, baseball is another thing if you're catching it on radio. And quite a different thing if you're catching it on radio today, when television sets abound, compared with catching it on radio in the pre-television years when there was no choice. And the differences on radio alone multiply depending on who's announcing.

Try listening to an announcer doing his three innings on television, and then tune him in for the next three on the radio. It's like different games.

And baseball is a different thing again when you're reading about yesterday's or last night's game in this morning's paper. To narrow the line of comparison: the latter is a different thing than reading the overtones and analysis of yesterday's game in this *evening's* paper, in which the columnists must discuss aspects, or analyze trends, other than providing mere journalistic reporting.

Furthermore, baseball is a different game depending on the different people you're discussing it with. And it's a different game depending on your own mood, condition, period of life, whereabouts, circumstances, et cetera. (It's also a different game in itself, objectively considering, in its own gradual changes.) It's reflected differently from numerous different angles: another testimony to the immense subjectivity of our inner lives, and the prevalence of relativity in myriad aspects. Baseball is a touch-stone to light up all our aspects, from all refracting points of view. But so is anything else a touchstone. But baseball is a good one, for it contains a system, a tradition, a history. There's plenty to work with there.

The Performer Engaged in His Action—Flowing into Art

The players in motion—running, pitching, throwing, fielding, hitting—are expressing some spontaneous aesthetic sensation while united with the larger forces of nature. Expending energy, they're in a different world from the observer; they're expressing emotion in a world of direct, participating sensations; they're part of their bodies over a larger field. The player is feeling something—exhilaration or whatever; the spectator identifies with him—happily but perhaps enviously. One is *performing* nature; the other appreciating. This comes within aesthetics but is hard to define. Grace, skill, or urgency of action, within playing rules, is close to art. Sport, somehow, is an active art form.

Perhaps its closest "pure art" neighbor is the dance. Sport is a series of improvisations, within a framework that "closes in" the game to its manageable unity. Informality combines with formality. It's theatrical, it's a "show." While in motion, it points toward a conclusion still unknown. The game "develops," as a play or dance does. Suspense, tension—familiar elements, to the theater. Baseball as theater: each performance (game) different. The actors in varying form, and in new combinations of possibilities. Each act is *toward* something: the action is forwarding. Inning by inning, a drama in the unfurling; play by play, pitch by pitch: it leads somewhere. The conclusion is held off, you have to *arrive* at it—through a series of events. The dance, the theater, music, and baseball are in *time*. And in the fullness of time, through moments of truth, the ripening picks up and the end comes in sight. That's *art*, when the end is "held off." A mere "score" is banal. It's in "how" that aesthetics includes baseball, in its collection of the beautiful.

Players Spaced Apart: Dull for Television Viewing?
But the Players Are Brought Closer by the Ball:
Though Body Seldom Conjoins with Body

Baseball doesn't appear to such good advantage on the key medium of our time, television, as do closer, more body-contacting, tighter-together sports like basketball, hockey, and football. The latter three are swifter of pace, with more compact action than the relatively slow lumbering baseball, with its players so widely spaced into areas of seemingly unrelated isolation. The action in baseball seems to be in stages; in those other sports, action seems dramatically all-at-once.

The slowness and deliberateness of baseball are related to the seemingly fixed, stationary points in the distances of fielders from each other in their positioning, and from the hitter. Spacing of performers affects the timing and connections between those performers. A "close play" at a base, a "tag" situation, are exceptions; baseball's flowing choreography is executed in pure, chaste, light, formal distances and angles from player to player on the field. The space positioning usually isolates the players, slowing the time intervals, as in a formal dance, stately, sedate. But sometimes the action compresses, and then you see a blurring fast together, in a flash of converging. The field shakes. The unexpected—or not quite expected—breaks the lulling rhythm of before.

In England, cricket resembles baseball in its few body contacts and in having a spacing-timing pattern different from soccer and rugby, which may be grouped with football, basketball, and hockey as friction sports of frequent body contact and specified time durations in which to complete a contest.

The Imaginative Faculty Decreased by Television Surplus

Baseball seems not to retain today the mythic importance it once had. Why this decline? One of the many possible reasons may be that television, in revealing so much, deprives us of a necessary *mystery* in which baseball used to be clad. There's less call upon the imagination. Thus underused, the imagination (source of mythic wonder and awe) may atrophy where baseball is concerned.

A point may have been reached where we know too much, we have too much information about what's going on, leaving no room for fantasy to rove and spin its thrilling emotional web.

In "the old days," clusters of people would wait around telegraphic offices or newspaper offices for slowly periodical "bulletins" to be posted up on the boards: latest score at the end of an inning, changing of a pitcher, name of hitter of home run just hit. Fans had to "work," with long waiting, diligence, for the little information they got: and when they got that little information through expenditure of effort and patience, they would cherish it, and lavish loving fantasy over it, embroidering it with *themselves*. There was so much they had to fill in through imagination: weaving the whole game together strand by strand, enchanting and captivating themselves. It was self-entertainment by dint of the labors of one's own mind. Their experience was thus personal, individual—not like today's impersonal and passive television reception, in which everything is swallowed ready-made and well analyzed, and you get more than you need to imagine with.

Formerly, with so much less *given*, the fan could work up a rich fantasy. Now, by comparison, in our age of incessant television, there's so *little* to be filled in through imagination. Imagination, in fact, becomes obsolete or redundant, and so can be easily discarded, with no seeming loss. Yet, the loss may be total.

In the early days of radio, there would be hypnotic ways of presenting people with baseball. The listener would have to "do the work" himself to make up for the increasingly well-known limitations of each broadcaster. A broadcaster would be an "imperfect vehicle," through whose very flaws in transmitting the game the avid listener had to "read in." Thus, there was *listener participation*: the listener was involved, for he had a necessary function, a needed capacity, to use, to compensate for the slim and flawed and spare "information" given.

The listener supplied and provided *from within* the deeper urgencies of reality. He helped to make a magical world. It was *his* world, special and personal, of baseball.

Nowadays, television does "all the work"—including taking us behind the scenes, to dugout and clubhouse interviews that dispel mystery through careful, literal, professional interviewing. We also have "debunking" books and articles, whose telltale revelations spill out the details that spoil a kid's love.

Love can be destroyed by the wrong kinds of "facts." Necessary illusions must be maintained for the valuable religious feelings of veneration, respect, awe, submission. "No man is a hero to his own valet." Now, every player is subjected to detailed scrutiny: he's "overexplained." His mystique (carefully protected in "the old days," like Babe Ruth's) is "explained away."

And that world becomes, thereby, reduced to factual, literal, mundane, nonmystery. And then—who would care anymore?

Overexposure—the communications media's way of doing a thing to death.

The middle-aged can recall "ticker-tape" broadcasts nostalgically. His team's game, at home or on the road, would be rained out. But the broadcaster in the studio or at the idle park in his booth would "reenact" and dramatize telegraphic information of another game in progress (especially a game "crucial" in a close pennant race) as it slowly came seeping in over the "wire." With his voice and imagination, he'd "bring it to life": embroidering outrageously—but often creatively—on the barest facts fed from that intermittent, staccato ticker. The listener would have to cooperate: imagining intensely, filling in those gaps with an equally pardonable poetic license.

The less known, the more "provided" by the receiver. The valuable contribution—the contribution which *creates* value. The mind "making" for itself what it takes into enjoyment. The exercise of a faculty because necessary. Now, alas, made redundant, obsolescent, in television's "overpowering" by ruthless, relentless detail. Crippling the looker into habitual passivity. Mechanical excess, depriving the mind.

The Whole Team, Feeding on Individual Talents

In baseball, as in other sport and non-sport activities, there's room on the same team for different kinds of physical specimens and specialists. A bulky, unwieldly, lumberingly unmaneuverable type may be cast as catcher or first baseman, where his deficiencies don't count so much; he compensates for his fielding immobility by sheer hitting power, and the balance would make him an asset on the squad. By contrast, a thin, wiry, light performer may make a great second baseman or shortstop with his flexible range and agility, while his lack of hitting power is partly offset by his speed.

Team "balance" consists of blending different types and skills, so that individual weaknesses are not so glaring in the overall combination, which has "enough of everything" to be a formidable aggregate—a *team*.

In basketball, the small back-court "playmaker" may well complement the tall, rangy center, and vice versa. A non-sports parallel: during the Second World War, midgets were in demand in airplane production for squeezing into narrow-angle corners of tails or fuselages of planes, otherwise inaccessible, to do riveting, bolting, welding, painting, et cetera.

The concept of "teamwork" derives from sports, and applies to any collective endeavor against some adversary—whether it be a national enemy, a natural disaster like earthquake or snowstorm, or commercial rival, or deadline, or challenge, or anything a "team" can operate against to overcome and conquer, as in a mountain or sea rescue operation or any other nonscheduled emergency.

Accompanying "teamwork" is the concept of the "sacrifice" of the individual for the sake of the whole, to "help" and "lend in" rather than "star." However, a "star" performance is usually the most cooperative "team effort" an individual can make—like a pitcher hurling a shutout. Of course, had it not been for those fielders behind him ...

Everybody "pitching in" in concert—the team thrives. But, as the extreme divergences in salaries can attest, some players simply add more than others—much more. Their contributions weigh in toward victory more consistently—and so they're the most rewarded. Teamwork, yes: but among unequals.

Sometimes the problem arises of the standout individual who does well for himself but who somehow in so doing, in so being, is a bad "team-man" and somehow does more harm than benefit for the team. Yet his individual performance, his record, his average—the competitive statistics—may exceed all the rest.

An example would be the star slugger who proudly refuses to bunt, or the "showboat" performer who pulls off spectacular grandstand antics but who in subtle ways, inaccessible to evidence, really "contributes" less than an unsung player with a more modest record. The latter may possess the "intangibles." But he may in less obvious ways win more games than the highly salaried superstar.

A temperamental individualist may daringly try to steal home in the clutch—and be out. It gets a huge rise from the crowd—they praise his being so spectacular, but it may cost the game.

Off the field, team morale may be upset by a temperamental individualist. The manager may pamper and indulge him overmuch; and everywhere else, such as in the press, this darling is accorded concessions that are denied to soberer players—who complain of "unfair" treatment. These off-the-field realities—such as a headstrong star being permitted to skip most of spring training or exercise sessions or batting practice —may be disturbing for the "togetherness" of the team.

A proud individual star on a brilliant home run streak may press for homers at times when just "getting a piece of the ball" may be more strategic. The team may resent him for putting himself ahead of it.

Or a tantrum may be thrown on the mound by a pitcher who doesn't want to be relieved—though the manager is relieving him for the *good of the team.*

Sometimes individual records and statistics come directly into contradiction with team welfare. A player may well be able to put his record above winning; it may be possible: at the team's cost. This is a grievous manager's problem.

Teamwork—but not at the cost of conformity and dullness that subdue unique styles and special talents. Sometimes the individualist *is justified*—he's got to do things *his* way, or fall not only from prominence and glory but even from team-boosting *quality*. That's the other side to this recurrent problem.

Specialists Before Us—The Watcher's Privilege

Showdowns of experts are intriguing. Champion chess player of all Russia versus champion chess player of all of the West. The heavyweight boxing championship. Australia's best tennis player versus America's. Each recognized expert is "bearing down." One of the antagonists, adversaries, combatants, must "give"—lose. The other prevails. The struggle is the drama.

Imagine in a Major League contest that classical confrontation, thrilling to contemplate, actual to watch, between pitcher and hitter. Natural opponents.

A single man is on the mound, whose expert specialty is pitching. He has funneled his whole life force and talent into that single application, by which he makes his living: it's his profession, and his whole livelihood, career, reputation, life's opportunity depend on how well he performs in this chosen occupation.

And he "bears down" with all his might, guile, resources, cunning, experience, all of his vocational training brought to bear in back of him, behind each pitch, against that single obstacle: the hitter.

His sole concentrated purpose in dealing with that hitter is to dispose of him, dispense with him, "get him out," "knock him off," send him back to the dugout.

It's specialist against specialist, equally determined. The pitcher is putting his life behind each pitch. He uses all his specialty to get rid of the hitter.

But the hitter, on *his* part, is just as much of a specialist. His livelihood depends on hitting. He carries with him to the plate a background of countless sweating hours of batting practice in batting cages. His goal: to do violence to the aforementioned pitcher, "take the bread out of his mouth." To defeat the pitcher, trounce him, knock him out of the box, send him to the showers—or the Minors, yet. To succeed, the batter must destroy the pitcher, dash the latter's hopes.

To succeed, the pitcher must destroy that batter. They press all their skills, bring all to bear against each other.

And you and everyone else are the witness. It's out in the open. The result will be *known*.

Locked in combat, best against best. That's the essence of drama.

Or *relatively* best against best. If not the World Series, it's a season contest. Or it's a Minor League game, but still the survival of the fittest, for only a small proportion of those who try can actually break into professional ball. Or it's a college match, but still it represents the cream of the crop of the respective student bodies who've "tried out" for the teams. Relatively, it's best against best, of all the pool of talent available and competing for "top" honors.

The spectator is all-privileged. And he gets the best for cheap. Especially at the Big League rate.

Here's an analogy from another field, a different sort of entertainment. You pay a few dollars, just a few dollars, to enter a movie theater. And, *just tor you* (seemingly—though it's really for many, many yous) is a film production that cost millions of dollars to produce! High-paid actors, the expensive talents of experienced directors, cameramen (their complicated gear, top-rate equipment), script writers, editors, script girls, secretaries, coordinators, distributors, managers—people of big jobs. All that highly concentrated, top-anxiety work by the top people in their high-powered, high-pressured, high-paid, highly specialized fields—all for *you* (seemingly). All for you. That's what it's like to be at a *Major League* ball game. The whole lives of the best Big Leaguers, with years of struggle, frustrations, culminating in success against huge cutthroat competition and forbidding odds, are placed before you for your privileged inspection—perhaps to incur your distaste, your disapproval—in any given play. An aggregate of the best talents and of lifetime devotions, at their respective primes, are on the field, in a performance; and you're there, having paid the price of admission. They want to beat each other's brains out, from opposite squads. They throw their all into it. Pitcher versus hitter, time and time again. This is drama that transcends its professionalism. It's pure and priceless, it's life—at a tiny admission price. There they are, the greatest of their era, doing the best they can. And you're judging them, and you're immersed in it! It's the baseball bargain of a lifetime. It's the golden metaphysics of life itself, focused on a field of play. And you're in the picture. They're there for you. Consecrated before you, the best physical endowments of the game. And you have your private view, judging them. You're the critic. You see the whole and the parts, the way you can. It's your way of seeing life itself. There's life, in the concentrate. Forces striving to win. The battling back, the coming from behind. The game, as a pageantry of sun and shadow, or under the lights. Live talents endeavor heroically for elusive prizes—before your very eyes. It's an experience encircled by every overtone of existence. This is your living, going by.

The Long Season Means Higher Drama, If...

The season is so long that, plowing through the monotony and fatigue that set in in the August dog-days for player and fan, is a building up of tension and suspense. A huge base is thus constructed upon which drama and importance are conferred on crucial late-season games as the pennant race "goes down to the wire" (*if* it does). The day-in and day-out of the long summer sets it all up, and can make the end of September thrilling, when the games "really count." (Actually, they *all* count.)

Thanks to the long-drawn-out season, decisive contests of the last two weeks of a close pennant fight are often the most exciting, dra-ma-laden, theatrically pulsating, bitterly scrapped-for, pressure-pop-ping, and truly climactic games known to baseball: more so than the World Series matches, since the World Series by comparison is so short and can be so suddenly determined; and infinitely more so than that mere exhibition spectacle, the semi-fraudulent "All-Star Game."

To draw a literary analogy: Aristotle said that, quality in other respects being equal, a long work of literature is superior to a short one. That's because the structure of interrelating parts being vaster in the good *long* work, every line in that work has more references and signifi-cant connections with the whole that supports it. Thus, Proust's lengthy, interminable *Remembrance of Things Past*, and Tolstoy's *War and Peace*, and Joyce's *Ulysses*, and Dante's *Divine Comedy*, and Homer's *Iliad* and *Odyssey* are extra-wonderful because of their epic builds. Each one has so much room to contain so much great stuff.

The same with the long baseball season. What a crescendo can cli-mactically derive from the spun-out, sheer laborious consecutiveness of day games, night games, and double-headers all the season long! It's an immense building-up—potentially. But if one team wins by a large mar-gin, there's somewhat of an anticlimax risked.

Same with a long literary work—the same risk is on, since massive-ness itself, monumental solidity, are no guarantees that enough passages in the work will give off the sparks of interest to bind fast the universal reader in a rhapsody of wonderment. Over the long haul, it's still the parts that count, as well. And the long season, when it comes down to it, is reduced to indivisible units: games.

No, these units *are* divisible: by innings. And each inning is divisible by each pitch. So the fleeting second of the ball's release and flight to the batter is the component elemental, through infinite multiplication, to the huge, intricate, complex, monumentally constructed, deviously winding season, with all of its everything jammed into it, or loosely packed, over the long, long summer.

Exercises in Baseball as a Way of Fiction

The following is a semi-surrealistic series of episodic baseball fictions, featuring a character called "my friend," and the first-person narrator—"my friend's" foil, rival, and alter ego. They trade tales, mostly, in compiling this conversational fiction sequence. It touches on baseball philosophically by route of all of life, valuing life, and ends up with the anti-despair of preserving it.

Baseball is one of life's reflectors. When fans talk baseball, they mean other things too. It's symbolic language, articulate of universals. It preciously contains correspondences and references to everything else included in life's non-baseball sphere. Thus, it opens out. It's a voice.

I played ball with my friend. He pitched. He batted. I watched. He won. That bolstered his ego. He got delusions of grandeur, like the mumps or chicken pox. It even affected his sanity, if any sanity remained after having been exposed to all the vicissitudes of his very uncertain life, fluctuating at a notorious level between up and down, with the up being always low and the down dropping out beneath him entirely. Such, in the long run, is life. If ever a guinea pig was human, the illustration lived to be my friend. There he goes. To a ball game. It might give him ideas. They'll clash with other ideas, but what the hell? Nobody is ruined more than he already is. Suffering turns to joy.

Although unathletic, my friend went to a ball game. He enjoyed it nevertheless, and pretended he had played. "But your name isn't in the paper," I wisely informed him, glancing at the latest sporting results. "I went under a pseudonym," said that modest athlete, "in order not to be mobbed into counterfeit autographing by literally worshipping fans. Tomorrow I'll take my bat and hit the ball again for another home run. Then, to spread the laurels, I'll change my name to a new ballplayer and win an equal democracy for both sides." "You're on no team?" I asked.

"I'm on every team," he said, and dominated the scene. I had to admire his courage. "But does the umpire upset you?" "Oh him? He doesn't count." "Then what's the score?" "Why are you so result-thirsty?" he retorted; "just enjoy the game." "Do you pitch as well?" I happened to ask. "Only when I'm at bat," he replied. "Then are you a star?" "Can't you read a record book?" he said, and then we began to get literary. The conversation switched to libraries. "Any book you happen to take out, I'm the author," he tipped me off. So he was intellectual as well. Renowned equally for the bat and the pen. Forgivably, I was awed.

"Is everybody like you?" I asked, and he said it depended on how many mirrors he could see at once sturdy enough to include his whole physique, the muscles outstanding on a bulging ego. His boasting bored me, so I asked for a story illustrating someone else's heroics. "Might it have psychiatric overtones," he asked, "to deepen its theme of baseball dimension?" I said why not, impressed with his attention to the mind. "It's about a pitcher," he said, "and the effect he had on the batters his deceiving curve had victimized; and what they do for compensation." "How interesting," I said. So, combining his baseball and literary style, he served up this oddball, twisting delivery, that tricked me as it fell across the plate:

"There was a pitcher kind of ballplayer. Although big and strong, he threw a very slow curve ball. The batters couldn't understand. After the game, they did research in the library, and studied psychology. Next time they faced this pitcher, they were completely adjusted to striking out, in a normal and nonneurotic way. As they returned to the dugout, they received a certificate of mental health. They also received a ticket to the Minor Leagues. To adapt themselves to the change, they became psychiatrists. Their mind developed, but their bodies sagged. Obese, and weighed down with a German accent, these former athletes specialize in sex ailments. Many a woman patient has jumped off the couch, and pronounced herself free. A policeman (an ex-umpire) would have to lock her up."

"That was a very entertaining story," I said, "but it has no moral." "Make one up then," the author of it said. "No, the moral is sure to be wrong," and I backed out. "It usually is," he shrugged, and promptly embraced nihilism. As nihilism is thin and empty, there was no warm sensuality out of that hug. "Go to Paris," I suggested. "No, I want to be where baseball is," he determined. Patriotism? No. Predilection.

"I can tell you a baseball story now," I said. "I'm in the groove, the mood," he abundantly welcomed. So I held the gloomy fate of a failed ballplayer in readiness. It was his fault, but the public magnified it. To serve him right, divine justice gave him blindness at the end. Or did blind justice offer him a divinity contract in the other League altogether? Our fates go fluctuating, and end up by being themselves fatally determined. "Tell it already, and stop eating your own prechewed philosophy," my friend gently cajoled. Had he read my own mind? How thoughtless of him! "All right! Batter up!" I said, and dusted off my home palate, while the batter's box became occupied by the doomed figure in spikes, straining his sight against his enemy stretched to uncoil the missile from his superior mound.

"A player hit the baseball, ran from base to base, but neglected to be safe in the final act of coming home. The audience hissed, and the reviews in the morning papers were atrocious. One critic, sick to his stomach, fouled up his own editorial. The public could barely contain its disgust. The player was voted out of office, and degraded to the position of umpire. He took up the art of wearing glasses, and even now, when he squints, blindness peers through."

"Too bad what happened," my friend commented. Out of respect, we paid a few seconds of silence. Then he said, "Can you keep talking about baseball? No other subject affords me any interest as that symbolic game." "Symbolic! What of?" I asked. "At least of itself, that's for sure," he said. "Damn your enigmas, your conundrums," I protested, upholding simplicity like a violet above the labyrinthine wilderness of a too-plush spring. "Okay," he conceded, "then just talk about baseball directly, without spreading it to other fields. Bet you overlap." "I'll stick to the sport itself," I defied, and began, resolutely, withdrawing all extraneous matter from my mind's baseball park, where only the game had to be played:

"A ballplayer threw a ball. A bat struck it. To delight gravity, it bounced. Then, loving mother nature, it rolled. The grass bent in its path. Out of energy, it stopped. The sun located the ball with a friendly ray. Another ballplayer, with a glove, picked it up. His performance made fielding history. The catch was known as a defensive gem. The umpire was struck dumb. The spectators plunged into applause, and lost their collective voice. They found it the next morning, while reading the sports page.

"Another ballplayer batted a ball. It flew over a fielder's head. The batter threw his bat away, and started to run. The action made him slide into third base. Panting with aggression, he was called safe. Embracing the smiling umpire, he felt like a true hero. The spectators unanimously agreed."

"I don't," my friend said. "You weren't there," I cut him. Chastised, he listened again. I got down to fundamentals. Even l could understand them. My friend listened for flaws. This unnerved me, and soon, as will be seen, I slid off into inferences, and lapsed into opinionation. My friend rooted me on.

"A catcher crouched. The pitcher threw. The batter missed. The catcher missed. His chest protector went 'oof.' No wonder he will become a wrestler.

"For a ball or a strike, or for safe or out, or for foul or fair, the umpire's impartial judgment is called upon. He exercises free will, or the right to choose a decision. He will never be elected to the Supreme Court. He often becomes blind, in order to clear away all doubt from his eyes. Then he buys a seeing-eye dog, to scare the ballplayers.

"When you watch baseball, keep your eye on the ball. Different players take turns at catching it. The object is to win. Bats and gloves are necessary equipment, as well as spikes. Spectators are known as fans. It is psychologically proven that they are frustrated ballplayers. Upon occasion, they boo."

"I think you embellished the pure sport with a few sideline moral tosses and judicial interpretations," said my friend smilingly; "so I win the bet." "Go to hell," I said, clearly pissed off: "Let's see you do better." "I intend to invest our great pastime with democratic implications, spiritual insights, and political overtones," said my friend, warming up emotionally to what, it became apparent, was his soul's favorite subject on earth:

"Baseball is an annual summer game. It is traditionally played by sunlit men. Their twinkling uniforms flash along the arc of a ball. The ball itself, contorted by the pitcher, is bruised by the bat. It bounds irregularly over the grass, or blurs the sky, until trapped by the hunting glove. As a baseball game ends, fans travel home with their hunger. But their dreams pursue the imaginary ball. The ball decides good and evil, and along its gambling path the unpopular umpire's Last Judgment concludes with triumph or with loss. While tragedy stalked Achilles, while demons unbalanced the ancient Lear mind, fate graced baseball with DiMaggio and Ruth. When the last boo, from the insane common man in the bleachers, clutters heaven with the echo, then let the dry bones of free men freely rot."

"But when will come that last boo, when will the dry bones of free men freely rot?" I asked, for baseball seemed destined to reign forever as America's truly national sport. "How I love the Yankees," I added. "Me too," adored my friend: "But as for your question, I can say that world destruction, for example from an atom bomb, has a good chance of ending baseball." "That would be totally terrible, an evil plight," I moralized, astounded that such an event was even possible. "It's incredible," I said; "men deserve to live." "You bet they do and us too," my friend reliably agreed. Here was harmony, between us. Would discord destroy it? Yes, the discord from without: international thermonuclear warfare. Soon we were alarmed. We scanned the skies looking for a sign.

"Are you scared of the atom bomb?" I asked my friend. "I can always duck," he replied, swaying his head off his flexible neck in illustration.

We like to put all idle theory to the proof, so we waited for a factual plane to appear. Finally, we saw one, miles high in a lazy blur off the top of the sky, but it went out of our vision without dropping an atom bomb. "We're at peace, that's why," said my friend, protecting his courage despite the serene safety that assailed us. True to summer, every tree was green.

We followed all the green, and wound up in the following spring. Being city boys, we sought nature in a park. And found children at their play. Watching them, we were they again, and time had melted difference away. The same ball we had stopped playing with, was now being bounced. It reminded us of our bruised childhood, our crippled youth, and antique infancy, all three of which were pleased to take place in the past, since our past was broad enough to contain them, wide enough to nourish their memories, and deep enough to recall their regret and furnish room for the expansion of nostalgia. One particular boy, or his ball, became the focus of an awful significance.

A little boy kicked a large rubber ball. It was really a globe of the world; I could see the continents, painted orange against the blue surface of the ball. "Be careful of the world," I cautioned. My friend butt in. "The world can take care of itself " he boasted, stepping on the ball. It exploded. "That was my crystal ball," he said, and rushed to phone a reporter. The little boy bawled. "Don't worry, I'll get you another world," I promised. The park filled with a chorus of its green trees.

Opera and Baseball: Audacity's Darlings, in Their Brother-Bond of Sheer Excess: Transcendent Transports into "Immature" Exuberance and Otherworldly Heights. The Fans' Delirious Communal

By perhaps more than coincidence, lots of opera lovers are baseball fans and vice versa. What do opera and baseball have in common? Both appeal to the intense, excessively romantic; they "pull out all the stops," they really "go to town." The aria is sheer, ecstatic, impassioned sound, for its own sake of wild beauty, audaciously full-throated. It's insane, really, it doesn't stand to reason; life just isn't that way, but art is. So it is, there's something inexplicably crazy about baseball: the violence with which the pellet is twirled by the controlled hurler; and the acrobatics of fielders in their lunging strides; the mayhem of a batter really taking a swipe. It seems all so childlike—or rather, adolescent. And adolescent, too, are those opera "plots." Adolescent are the sobbing sounds that tremor and blast their way out of well-trained throats and chests; adolescent are the libretto lyrics; the whole thing is "immature." *Intensity*, in fact, is "immature." That's why baseball is lovable: it vindicates immaturity, it justifies it, the rules call for it, in intense competition. *Running hard* from home to first is like the utter, outlandish abandon of the aria being hurled, blasted out, beyond the back row of the dark opera house from that overdramatically-lit stage. It's all so "too much." The "too much" is just that extra little thing needed. Without it, there's *not enough*, for the baseball, or for the opera, connoisseur.

The singer and the athlete, strutting in their playlike cages to the wild acclaim of the audience. Strutting like spoiled, precocious brats who, however, are assured that their each gesture and chord, stance and vowel, reflex and tone, are calculatedly "just right"—they "bring down the house." Oh, that applause! Oh, the fees! Prima donnas, exulting in glory. The big scene overdone, "playing to the grandstand." Encores galore.

The singer "belts out" the aria, full-blast. The batter belts that ferociously flung pellet and belts it in full, it's the mighty swat. It breaks up the game. It's way "out of there."

The glory. The performer's well-pampered narcissism. It's a crowd-pleaser.

The crowd is overwhelmed with exuberance. The crowd goes home glowing. "There's nothing like it," says the opera lover, the baseball lover, shaking his head, bewildered, to himself, thinking of opera or of baseball. "Nothing like it in the world." Naturally. It's *out* of the world. The world is too tame a place to confine it, so it roars, or stretches, outside. Those wonderful sounds, those wonderful baseball spectacles, derive from an otherworldly melody, from ethereal harmonics. No use trying to be technical about this. Sure, the technical explains *part*-way. But, as the Elizabethan Francis Bacon once put it, "There's no beauty without some strangeness in the proportion." It's weird, that's all. It's weird.

Shaking his head, sadly. He meant, "It was wonderful," but the intensity of his feeling reduced him to the obligation of an understatement: "it's too much," it's "really something."

He shakes his head sadly, on his way home by car, subway, or bus. Why so sadly? Because he just got a slice of heaven, which is echoing in his head-chamber, and reverberating down to his chilly bones of mortality. It was all "too wonderful." He feels grim, he's headed back to the workaday world, to fact and plainness. Opera and baseball had liberated an immense *fantasy*. Hence, their *fans*.

Shaking his head, sadly. It was too good to last. If only life or the world could be that way *all the time*. But life and the world are pedestrian, mundane. Such peaks, such exuberant flights, such soaring dimensions as just enraptured him are "not for this world." They're confined to the opera house, to the baseball park, like rare exotic canaries of wild plumage caught from some South American paradise. It's all "too good to be true." So, by the *world's* terms, it's just "not true." It has truth to *itself* (to baseball or opera). But it's sure not "true to life." Thank God for that! Life would be unbearable, if it were *always* like what was just witnessed or heard.

Melodies from heaven. Sound pouring down from infinity. The thundering fast ball, the solid crack, the line-drive base hit, really *drilled*. Perfection, excellence. Admirable!

No, leave life alone, let life be ordinary. The ordinary's place is in life. For the *extraordinary*, there are *special occasions*. So special, you even have to buy tickets in advance sometimes. "Next month, *Don Giovanni* is at the Metropolitan Opera House, all sold out, of course, but I reserved my seat early. I'll live in plain life till then. Then, that night, I'll simply ascend. Mozart will *transport* me."

Such "transports" were the wild heart-flutterings into love and paradise, as the word was used in English verse and prose centuries ago. It pertained to "rapture" and "enchantment."

The *special occasion*: at the opera. Or at the ballpark, in the *crucial series* of this tight pennant race. "Their ace against our ace, two big righthanders on the mound. We're two games behind. We can't afford to lose."

Taken out of life. "Out of this world," as Baudelaire implored; the poet wanted to go "out of this world." In opera and baseball peaks, we *are* thus "transported." In a fit of flight, then sadly thrust back again, to serve out our sentence in the world's prison of the commonplace; making the opera lover or baseball lover shake his head sadly on his way home from the show, the game, the event. The world shrinks back into its perfectly normal size. Hence the sadness, in the transition from supreme height to the "leveling off" into the ordinary, like "post-coitus" sadness, the melancholy following the orgasm. "It was great. Oh, well. It couldn't last. Here I am. Back again. I'm my 'normal self.'"

The sublime is for rare occasions. It's too wild to domesticate. But "professionals" can *deliver* some reasonable proxsimile of the sublime *consistently*. It's their high-paid job to. The opera and the baseball star have a great record of sustaining heights. They reach those high notes to pour down the sentiments from the heavens on us: we're drenched. Oh well, we asked for it. We wanted it, didn't we?

"The Sunday baths of the soul," in Wallace Stevens's phrase. When, with utter abandon (there being no work or obligation on Sunday), we sing and sing to our hearts' content, in the delightful privacy of the bathtub, and splash ourselves merry. We're swept into the skies of exhilaration.

Rare moments. The golden curtain lifts, or the velvet one opens, to reveal the stage set after the orchestra has just pumped out the overture. There's the fat, absurdly dressed singer in an old-fashioned costume; it's simply ludicrous—but we *believe*. Because we're *devout*. Here are his peals. The melody is coming over us, it's beautiful—it's agonizing. It's over, great applause. There's the soprano. What a note! How shrill, it's divine, such quavering. She's shrieking now. Well, I'm not at the opera house. This is heaven. Why not? I paid for it, didn't I?

There we are at the ballpark. Set the scene (like opera scene-set). That lovely sward of green. After the national anthem with everybody compulsorily standing in pious attention, it's "Batter up." "Here's the first pitch. It's *in there*, for a called strike. There's ball one, low and outside. There's a smash! The third baseman gloves it! Nice play! Throw to first ... in time! One out. Nice and brisk. Come on, you're working on a no-hitter, now."

"Take me out to the ball game/Take me out with the crowd ... For it's *one, two, three* strikes, you're out/At the *old—ball—game!*"

On the way home. The crowded subway; holding on to the straps while the train sways noisily from black station to black station. "Well, that was a nifty win. Now, we're only one behind, with four games left. We're in good shape. We just can't afford to lose now."

"Transports," pertaining to love. Love, from the breast. Love, at the heart of every opera plot. Love, that, in Dante's Italian, "Moves the sun and the other stars."

Love, *from* the heart, is at the heart of all things good and true. Man helps out nature's dearth or worldly deficiency, by making art, with its rounded-out abundances.

Opera is laden with abundances. Baseball is another art, an athletic improvisation by eighteen men at a time. The object is to win. But it's *how* the game goes, that's how. It's in *getting there*, that's the trick. The fun is *on the way*: like journeying to a place, with the journey being the thing, and not the getting there.

"On route to his win ... " "On route to the end of the opera ... " But *in between*: oh, what merry stops!

You're all there, the audience is at one. They're bound together with the same bond—of all being gripped by the same dramatic moment, the hush of suspense, the stillness of tension, the rumble of anticipation. They're all bound in to the same moment at the same place, under the same spell. It's the situational drama focused on that instant, a show-down. The feeling, "This is it." It's all come down to this, all that went before (in this opera, in this game—or in this season): and now comes the impact. It's the translucent timeless eternity, the very "moment of truth," when the action compacts, becomes richly condensed, at this critical juncture. Everybody was waiting for this without knowing it. Without *absolutely* realizing it, they're under an absolute compulsion, dominated by this central instant in a narrative time plot. That's art, or religion, at the *core*. That's life's "taking off."

"That's what it's all about," we say, in our seat at the opera or the game. And the stranger in a neighboring seat knows just what we mean. We didn't even have to say it. But we didn't want to let the luxury go by, of the rarity of feeling, for once, *un*alienated in this civilization. All mankind were brothers just then. We truly understood each other, all being charged with the same energy, the same message or signal from the same situation undergone purely in common. And that's not com-mon. The sudden end of a long war, or some Presidential assassination, or city-wide fire or earthquake disaster, or the Second Coming by Christ, or the End of the World in imminence—those bring men together as one. It's like a migration of thousands of birds in perfect flight coordina-tion, symmetrical formation, every feather in place and a place for every feather in that marvelous unison: each pulse synchronized to each other pulse of the whole flock, with incredible machine precision. That's one time individuality needn't be jealous or fear for itself, or begrudge the group and defy the group. Vital self-fulfillment *is* in the collective, just then.

The herd instinct *can* be enriching, when the experience is sublime, and natural. Under the heightened conditions of Art (including opera and baseball), such an event is possible to take place. That all-embracing electricity that fires up everyone to be stirred by the same current. A feeling of total Belonging.

The theater audiences in classical Athens were as one; they understood perfectly, in great unison, every motion on the stage, and each word got the same reception in them all. How fortunate were those playwrights, operating under such ideal conditions! Compare to the present, and you'll envy them on behalf of today's frustrated playwrights, who feel as if they don't have a chance, with communications all broken down. Pity them. The baseball player and the opera singer are more fortunate, for *their* audiences are prepared with the right language for perfect reception: the language is standard to the peculiar art of opera, or to the peculiar art of baseball; so when the right moment occurs in dramatic presentation in either of those media, the loss is minimal, and the whole throb is exactly transmitted—intact. We all "get it."

At that certain key moment: when all the action rushes together into a single time, from the whole pennant race, or the whole game, or the whole three-hour opera: It all comes crashing down, or gets stunningly resolved. The place is uncanny: the hush, the buzz, the flash runs through every spectator-participant there. "I wouldn't have missed it," they say later. "Not for my life."

It was drama, and it hinted as to the meaning of life. It didn't "give away" life's mystery, but there sure was illumination! It was unmistakable, however ambiguous. Something really happened. All the witnesses could testify—they were at the event. Now, *that's* an *event*: It didn't just "take place."

Life's meaning is somewhat hinted at there but remains, on the whole, vague. In one instant, we were all lifted up. We were afforded some "glimpse." Then we were set down again, where, here we are: the same people as before—not quite. There's something we can't forget—we really *went through* it, to get there. Then, it "happened."

A Structure for Containing the Miraculous and Grading Mysteries, a System of Revelation by Degrees: Baseball's Universe

The light, perfect structure or self-contained system of baseball allows certain mysteries of life to become recognizable and tangible, by setting them off from the way they are in real life.

(By "mysteries," I mean things like the simple, daily miracles of motion, reflex, and coordination: converted in baseball to the fluently complex operations of running, catching, throwing, hitting, et cetera. Plus, the law of gravity that makes a baseball drop down out of a blue sky; the amazingness of distance, such as the distance between home plate and the outfield grass; the amazingness of trajectories, of balls hit "where"; the amazingness of the properties of the "bounce," et cetera: what makes a ball stop bouncing and just roll, eventually dwindling to inertia? Physics is amazing. The physical performances of athletes are too.)

In real life we're always personally touching the mysteries, so we don't actually see them, we're too involved in the sea of them, surrounded by the sea of them. In baseball, they're "all there" in the recognizable structure.

So it is in art. Things fall into place and are seen by degrees and proportions, within the frame of a painting, within the form of a story. A network's pattern appears, the self-enclosed world emerges, in a poem, when the poet has "put it all together." Proust's *Remembrance of Things Past*, Joyce's *Ulysses*, Tolstoy's *War and Peace*—each is a self-contained, particular yet universal, world.

Likewise, a team can "put it all together," when everything seems to work in harmony as a unity: when that happens, the team wins the pennant.

"Putting it all together" can also be done by an individual performer. Take a given pitcher: on some days his fast ball is humming, but his curve is missing the corners or is floating up too high. Other days his curve might be sharp, but his fast ball might lack its "hop." Or his "stuff" on a given day may be great, but unfortunately his control may be "off." But when he "puts it all together"—then that's a game well pitched!

All that seems self-evident. But the borderline is thin—nonexistent, often—between the all-too-obvious and the incredible, the miraculous. What we take for granted borders on the inconceivable. The inconceivable is what's most worth conceiving. The world plays tricks before us. Baseball is an open world. Its tricks confuse, enlighten, obscure, illuminate, simultaneously. We're awake, to its dream.

The One Constant, Gliding in Our Midst

Baseball goes on, essentially unaltered, though the nation itself goes through violent historical upheavals and the times are always changing. Violence is on the land today. But the game of baseball remains its peaceful self. It's constant, enduring, and links the century together in our land—the twentieth century, when so much happened and baseball remained essentially placid in the midst of all. It's dependable, and goes on. Fashions come and go, and wars, and social problems, economic crises, political climates. Baseball outlives them all—in our midst. A steady constant that retains its own slow unfolding patterns, while convulsions grip the land outside and tear out the old to plant in the new. Baseball serenely glides by—permanent, beautiful, ever itself: insular, yet mildly reflecting, in a peaceful way, in its own terms, the changes going on outside. The world's cataclysms come about, and subside. But every summer is played the same eternal baseball game. We can time our lives, to its peaceful eternity. We can trust to its repose, and security. It's always going on.

Acknowledgments

The publisher thanks the following individuals for their generous financial support which helped to defray some of this book's production costs:

Ross Barkan
Brian R. Boisvert
Shane Jesse Christmass
Jason Crane
Remembering old Joe DiMaggio throwing that first pitch, Deborah & Peter
Steve Elsberry
Maureen Crowley Heil
Haya K.
Alvin Krinst
Arthur P. Larkin
Larry Luddecke
Sidney McMahon
Mark S. Mitchell
Colin Myers
Father & Daughter, Greg & Hailey Pryor
Matthew J. Rogers
Michael Roznik
Roger O. Thornhill

About the Author

Marvin Cohen is an American essayist, novelist, playwright, poet, humorist, and surrealist. He is the author of nine published books and several plays. His short fiction and essays have appeared in more than 80 publications, including *The New York Times, The Village Voice, The Nation, Harper's Bazaar, Vogue, Fiction, The Hudson Review, Quarterly Review of Literature, Transatlantic Review,* and New Directions annuals. His 1980 play *The Don Juan and the Non-Don Juan* was first performed at the New York Shakespeare Festival as part of the Poets at the Public Series. Staged readings of the play have featured actors Richard Dreyfuss, Keith Carradine, Wallace Shawn, Jill Eikenberry, Larry Pine, and Mimi Kennedy.

Born in Brooklyn in 1931, Cohen has described himself as one who has "risen from lower-class background to lower-class foreground." He studied art at Cooper Union but left college to focus on writing, supporting himself with a series of odd jobs including mink farmer and merchant seaman. He also taught creative writing at The New School, the City College of New York, C.W. Post of Long Island University, and Adelphi University. Cohen currently lives in New York City with his wife, a retired paperback editor.

Of this, his first non-fiction book, he reports, "Baseball and life are ways of seeing each other. If the seeing is really done, both gain."

CPSIA information can be obtained
at www.ICGtesting.com
Printed in the USA
BVHW041407150719
553456BV00014B/446/P